ACCESS AND EXCELLENCE:
75 YEARS OF LONG ISLAND UNIVERSITY

THE BROOKLYN BRIDGE • SEPTEMBER 11, 2001

"I assume the presidency of this university committed to the fundamental premise that through learning and self-discovery we provide each generation with the capacity to know itself and the world around it; to search for that which is beautiful in life; and to realize what it means to be embedded historically, intellectually and culturally in time and space."

— David J. Steinberg,
inaugural address,
November 13, 1985

Library of Congress Control Number: 2001097323

ISBN: 0-913252-01-8

© 2001 Long Island University
700 Northern Boulevard, Brookville, New York 11548 • www.liu.edu

EDITOR:
Christopher T. Cory

DESIGNER:
Stephen Hausler
University Creative Director

ARCHIVIST:
Janet Marks
University Archivist

MANAGING EDITORS:
Doris Meadows

Kim Volpe
Assistant University Director of Public Relations

PROJECT DIRECTOR:
Paola Curcio-Kleinman
Associate Vice President of Marketing and Public Relations

Richard W. Gorman
Vice President for University Relations

ACCESS AND EXCELLENCE:
75 YEARS OF LONG ISLAND UNIVERSITY

LONG ISLAND UNIVERSITY PRESS
BROOKLYN • BROOKVILLE • SOUTHAMPTON

To the students of Long Island University,

past, present and future …

CONTENTS

FOREWORD
by Mary M. Lai B'42 3

CHAPTER ONE
Campuses 5

CHAPTER TWO
Intellectual and Cultural Life 27

CHAPTER THREE
A History 55
by Maren Lockwood Carden, Ph.D. and
Susan E. Dinan, Ph.D.

CHAPTER FOUR
Personalities 93

CHAPTER FIVE
Student Life 113

A Note on Sources 148

Acknowledgements 149

Index 151

The official seal of Long Island University incorporates a tradition of symbolism that universities have used since medieval times. Around the perimeter is the University name in Latin and its founding date. Also in Latin, the language of academic heraldry, is the University motto: "Urbi et Orbi" ("On Behalf of the City and the World"). Borrowed from the Pope's bi-annual blessing, the reference was meant to expand and ennoble the new nonsectarian university's mission: to open its doors to all who qualify without discrimination by race or creed; to provide not only an education for one's life work, but a broader understanding of the whole of life; to prepare students for a place in the community and inspire a sense of responsibility for the general good. The scallop shells and rippling waves connote the seas surrounding Long Island and the harvest they yield. The center is the open book of learning.

FOREWORD

The die was cast for us, and now, more than half a century later, we look back on personal and professional lives that have been inextricably linked with Long Island University.

A Life and a University Entwined

My future was set in 1939. It was then, with scholarships offered to me by both Long Island University and New York University, that I opted to attend Long Island University. It was a wonderful decision for many reasons. Most important, that's where I met my husband, Buck B'41 (see page 110). In 1946, four years after my graduation as an accounting and economics major, President Tristram Walker Metcalfe offered me the job of bursar, which at that time meant becoming the chief business officer of the University. One year later, President Metcalfe made another call, this time offering Buck a faculty position. The die was cast for us, and now, more than half a century and many job titles later, we look back on personal and professional lives that have been inextricably linked with Long Island University.

These years have been blessed for me. The growth of my family and the growth of the University paralleled each other. Ultimately my two sons also obtained degrees from Long Island University. Through and through, we've been a Long Island University family.

I started working at the University at a time when women did not often hold positions of great professional responsibility. In fact, in the early days I was frequently asked: "How does it feel to be in a man's job?" To that I've always responded that a job doesn't have a gender. There have been times when being a woman worked against me as I was ignored as the only woman in a meeting; in other instances I found that bringing womanly qualities to bear in negotiating thorny issues tended to resolve those issues to the benefit of the University.

Often, the needs of the University have had a strong impact on my personal life. During the early 1960s, for instance, when enrollments soared and significant governmental funding was available for expansion, the University experienced exhilarating highs that also presented me with serious personal challenges. Though my children were young, as the person charged with overseeing the construction of the many buildings rising on our three campuses, my work days extended around the clock. As I dealt with architects, contractors, change orders and furnishings, my good health, faith and the support of my husband and extended family kept me going.

My own commitment to my life and work at Long Island University has never been an issue for me. Over 59 years I have witnessed the growth of a truly remarkable institution. I'm sure the best is yet to come.

I've been an integral part of a university whose mission of access and excellence I cherish, an institution that makes a difference in the lives of its students because of the dedication of its faculty and staff. It's been more than five decades, but I've never seriously entertained the idea of leaving or retiring. My life is right here, as it has been since 1946. I am delighted that the University's 75th anniversary and this book are providing a chance to share the struggles and triumphs of our history with the members of our University family and the world at large.

Mary M. Lai

Mary Maneri Lai, Long Island University's vice president for finance and treasurer, received a bachelor's degree in 1942 and an honorary doctorate in 1986 from the Brooklyn Campus. In 1996, the University's finance building was named in her honor.

"The University can be justifiably proud of its growth into one of the largest and most comprehensive private universities in the U.S."

— Middle States Association
of Colleges and Schools, 1993

CHAPTER ONE
CAMPUSES

The restored former lobby of the Brooklyn Paramount Theater, recently named the Eugene & Beverly Luntey Commons, houses the Brooklyn Campus student union.

Marjorie Merriweather Post's gracious Hillwood mansion, now Gary Winnick House, is the administrative center of the C.W. Post Campus.

The fabled beaches of Long Island's East End attract local residents, tourists from around the globe and students from Southampton College.

Students relaxing beneath "The Arch," the icon of the Brooklyn Campus.

The domes and weathervanes of C.W. Post are skyline sentinels that lend distinction to several campus buildings.

Once it ground grain and corn for the local economy. Now this colonial-era windmill (c. 1715) is the widely recognized symbol of Southampton College.

Aerial walkways provide all-weather access to most buildings at the Brooklyn Campus.

The University's Rose and Gilbert Tilles Center for the Performing Arts, located on the C.W. Post Campus, is recognized as Long Island's premier showplace for a huge variety of concerts and dance events. The Center opened in 1981 with a performance by the New York Philharmonic, which has returned each season.

During the spring of 2001, an abandoned MTA substation gave way to a gleaming tower of education. Six glass-sheathed stories high, the Jeanette and Edmund T. Pratt Jr. Center for Academic Studies is home to new facilities for the School of Education, the Honors Program and the Higher Education Opportunity Program at the Brooklyn Campus.

The Brentwood Campus, one of three University regional campuses, pioneered Fast-Track master's degree programs to accelerate working professionals' studies.

The University's northernmost location, the Rockland Graduate Campus, offers master's degrees and advanced certificate programs.

Administrative activities at Southampton College are centered in Southampton Hall, originally designed as a private home by architect Grosvenor Atterbury.

Originally built by the renowned architect John Russell Pope in 1927, C.W. Post's Lorber Hall was once home to financier W.E. Hutton. (His cousin E.F. Hutton lived a stone's throw away in what is now the Fine Arts building.) Recently refurbished, the stately mansion boasts "smart" classrooms, a lecture hall and a library. It houses the School of Professional Accountancy and the popular Hutton House Lectures.

Students find a shady urban oasis on the Brooklyn Campus.

Picnics to protests, orientation to graduation — the Great Lawn at C.W. Post.

Chancellors Hall, a $10 million academic center, houses classrooms, labs, a lecture hall, WPBX-FM broadcasting facilities and faculty offices at Southampton College.

This architect's rendering will soon become a reality. The Jeanette and Edmund T. Pratt Jr. Recreation Center at C.W. Post, scheduled to open in spring 2002, will hold an eight-lane, collegiate-competitive swimming pool, a three-court basketball arena, an indoor jogging track, racquetball courts and aerobics and weight rooms.

The B. Davis Schwartz Memorial Library on the C.W. Post Campus offers access to the 2.75 million-volume University library system.

A bird's-eye view – C.W. Post's magnificent 307.9-acre campus is just 45 minutes from Manhattan.

The Westchester Graduate Campus, now located at Purchase College of the State University of New York, has offered degree programs in education, business administration, health administration, industrial pharmacy and health science for more than 25 years.

The Brooklyn Campus proudly flies the flags of each of its schools above bustling downtown streets.

Brooklyn's signature EAB Clock Tower distinguishes the Zeckendorf Health Sciences Center that houses facilities for nursing, pharmacy, and health sciences.

India is one of seven international "campuses" for the University's Friends World Program students. Here, one gazes at the Taj Mahal from the Red Fort in Agra.

"The most exciting place,

where students were desperate to learn."

— Professor Robert Spector, Ph.D. B'49,
Director of Humanities and Communications,
Fine and Performing Arts, Brooklyn Campus

CHAPTER TWO

INTELLECTUAL AND CULTURAL LIFE

Memories

"The guts award"

Among the significant developments during the half-century since the founding of the [George Polk] Awards has been the increase in criticism of the press. The litany of complaints, much of it originating from the fourth estate itself, includes indictments of reporting as trivializing, biased, vulgar, mean-spirited, malicious, self-serving and inaccurate. To those of us who have been participating in the selection of Award winners, these assessments seem based on much too narrow a sample of the performances and achievements of our nation's press. When the scope is broadened, we find reporters monitoring diverse beats from city hall to the environment, health care to racial justice, wars to world markets, as they continue to be the indispensable watchdogs for the public interest.

The Polk Awards memorialize George Polk, a CBS correspondent slain covering a civil war in Greece in 1948. At the suggestion of his family, the Polk Award committee posts the names of all journalists who died in pursuit of a story during the previous year. The list continues to be much too long.

Among the Polk Award recipients in 1997 was the book, "Requiem," a collection of photographs by 135 journalists who died covering wars in Southeast Asia from 1950 to 1975. Their dedication and sacrifice is identified with George Polk and inspires these Awards as a standard and legacy.

— Sidney Offit H'99, Curator, George Polk Awards

The Polk Awards, launched by the University in 1949 to honor excellence in investigative journalism are known to reporters as the "guts award," and rank among the most prestigious prizes in journalism. Left to right: President Albert Bush-Brown, Don McNeill and Dan Rather of CBS News and curator Sidney Offit at the 1983 ceremony.

Journalists Killed in the Line of Duty in 2000.

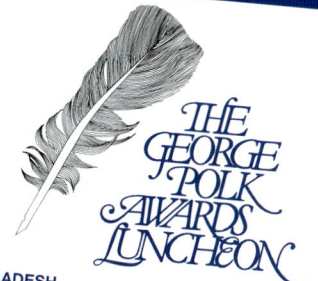

THE GEORGE POLK AWARDS LUNCHEON

BANGLADESH
Mir Illias Hossain
Shamsur Rahman

BRAZIL
Zezinho Cazuza

COLOMBIA
Juan Camilo Restrepo Guerra
Gustavo Rafael Ruiz Cantillo
Alfredo Abad Lûpez

GUATEMALA
Roberto Martinez

HAITI
Jean Léopold Dominique

INDIA
Pradeep Bhatia

MOZAMBIQUE
Carlos Cardoso

PAKISTAN
Sufi Mohammad Khan

PHILIPPINES
Vincent Rodriguez
Olimpio Jalapit, Jr.

RUSSIA
Vladimir Yatsina
Aleksandr Yefremov
Igor Domnikov

SIERRA LEONE
Saoman Conteh
Kurt Schork
Miguel Gil Moreno de Mora

SOMALIA
Ahmed Kafi Awale

SPAIN
José Luis Lûpez de la Calle

SRI LANKA
Mylvaganam Nimalarajan

UKRAINE
Georgy Gongadze

URUGUAY
Julio César Da Rosa

Information provided by the Committee to Protect Journalists (CPJ).

BROOKLYN CAMPUS
LONG ISLAND UNIVERSITY

Every Polk Awards ceremony reminds guests of journalists who lost their lives in pursuit of a story during the preceding year.

A return engagement for Billy Taylor — musician, inspiration, professor.

I was pleased to read that Billy Taylor will be joining your faculty at C.W. Post. I brought Mr. Taylor to the Brooklyn Campus in 1956 as part of a series of afternoon jazz programs I was producing in association with the Long Island University Jazz Club I organized in 1955. I met Mr. Taylor at the Composers, a swank supper club on 56th Street. He agreed to play solo piano and take questions from students in the student lounge, a venue where, with the cooperation of the administration, we presented evening concerts, always with the intention of enlightening young people about the music at a time when the full force of rock 'n' roll was clearing the air of jazz on radio.

After graduation I became a history teacher for 32 years in the New York City public school system, where I continued to present jazz musicians as performers and educators. Mr. Taylor started it all in 1956.

— John Doria B'57

Memories

Billy Taylor, performing on the Brooklyn Campus in 1956. Inset: In 2000 with philanthropist Rose Tilles, whose family endowed the Rose Tilles University Professorship in the Performing Arts which he inaugurated.

At Southampton College, students can work alongside nationally known radio professionals at WPBX-88.3 FM, a National Public Radio affiliate and flagship station of the Long Island University Public Radio Network.

Training in the written word has always been among the strengths of the Brooklyn Campus. Professor Emanuel Perlmutter (second from right), who was a reporter for The New York Times, is shown at a Brooklyn courthouse with a group of journalism students.

Clockwise from top: poets Langston Hughes and Marianne Moore; Holocaust survivor Elie Weisel; Senator and presidential candidate Hubert H. Humphrey; and General Douglas MacArthur — just a few of the leading figures in public and cultural life who have participated in events at the University's campuses.

Famed author, essayist and commentator Roger Rosenblatt, a member of the East End's vibrant literary community, has been instrumental in shaping the English & Writing program at Southampton College.

A poetic premiere for the screenwriter of "Goodfellas"

Nicholas Pileggi B'56 was known in college for poetry. His first published work is shown here. In years to come he became more widely known for his dialogue and prose. A successful screenwriter and author, his works include films like "Goodfellas," which he based on his best-selling novel "Wise Guy."

Adonis is a river,
Uprooting rock and washing stone,
Bathing fossiled women propped on polished bone,
Basking other ancients squatting by the sea,
Bound and twisted like a winterized tree.
Lying with their feet flaked beneath the snow,
Lamenting Stygian shores for reveries they know
Of suckeled suckling leaches, funnel-mouthed and fat
Beneath a fifty watt bulb of a rail-road flat;
And curled about a porcelain pot
Chipped in the corner of an empty lot,
Spurting from the nozzel of a garden hose
Was the dried-out remnant of a withered rose.
Enough to watch them starve
While squeezing from a shell
Curled yellow cream to carve
Christ's entrance into Hell.

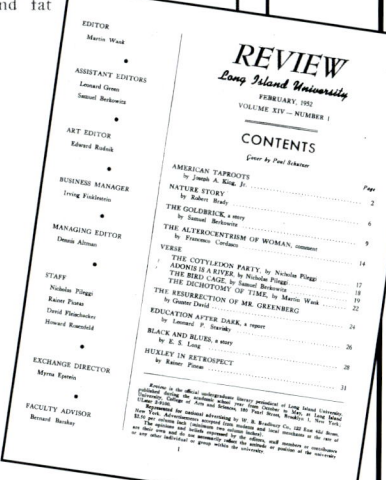

Upon this ancient stone where all men sit like sphinx
In the realized realization of those "muttering retreats,"
I watched a piece of paper float about the street,
Slash it's head upon the curb, and softly fall asleep.

adonis is a river
NICHOLAS PILEGGI

Brooklyn dodging

When we attended LIU the main campus was on Pearl Street in the Con Edison Building, across from Brooklyn Law School. Other classes were held at the YMCA close to the Academy of Music, as well as in the old Brooklyn Eagle Newspaper Building (no longer standing), plus rented spaces. I remember the Eagle building as having the oldest elevators in existence: close the door, pull on a heavy rope to start and pull again to stop!

One funny incident I do remember ... We had time to walk between classes when we had to leave Pearl Street to go to the Y for another class. One day we had time before going to Bob Spector's English class to grab a beer across from the Y building. A few of us went in, had a couple of beers and suddenly remembered our English class. We ran up to Dr. Spector's class trying to think of a good excuse — except he was glancing out of a window and could see us dashing out of the bar.

Robert Spector as a young professor.

— Lloyd Newman B'52

Memories

An extravagant start

A few years ago I attended the dedication of the Charles Zwicker Lobby of Lorber Hall at the C.W. Post Campus. It had been more than 30 years since I had seen Charlie Zwicker and at least 35 since I had worked for him as a novice accountant at Rosenblum and Zwicker. As a student in several of his accountancy classes I had been intimidated by Charlie's quick wit, Spartan-like manner and fiscal conservatism or, as some might say, his frugality.

However, I actually looked forward to reintroducing myself and reminiscing about old times. After sharing some fond recollections, I asked, "Charlie, do you remember how much you paid me when I began working for you?"

"No, how much?" he responded.

"I think I started out at 60 bucks a week."

In a tremulous voice, he indignantly exclaimed, "Impossible, I could never have been that extravagant!"

I guess the years haven't changed Charlie all that much!

— Stanley Barshay P'60,
retired senior vice president,
American Home Products and
trustee of Long Island University

Memories

Charles Zwicker, professor of accountancy, was a fixture at the C.W. Post Campus from 1957-1982. In addition to his work in the classroom, he served as dean of the School of Professional Accountancy from 1973-1980.

C.W. Post professor Stefan Wolpe was a member of the international community, composing avant-garde music for the 20th century. His work has been championed by such influential musicians as Peter Serkin, but his students treasured him for his eccentricities. Cynthia Lenox P'63, said: "There was never a dull moment in his class. He was a wild, crazy character who inspired all of us with his love of music." Wolpe is shown in this campus photo with Winthrop Palmer, a poet, writer and critic who taught at Post and Southampton and who, with her husband Carleton, a former University trustee, donated the funding that resulted in the Palmer School of Library and Information Science.

A generation of Southampton College music students fondly recall their training under Colonius Davis, an associate professor.

The celebrated cartoonist and author Jules Feiffer H'99, who teaches "Humor and Truth" in the Master of Fine Arts program in English & Writing at Southampton College, humorously shared the truths of teaching with readers of Long Island University Magazine.

In the converted cow barn of the old Post estate, students unravel the mysteries of chemistry.

Among the most beloved of personalities in the early days of Long Island University was the elegant Mildred Loxtin Barritt de Barritt, who served the University from 1929 until her retirement in 1969. In 1931, when she was named dean of women, she became the University's highest ranking woman. An individual of uncommon wisdom and wit, this teacher of English and American drama was valued as a warm and gracious counselor to faculty and students alike.

Bob Brier, professor, famed Egyptologist and host of award-winning documentaries, shares the wonders of ancient Egypt with students at C.W. Post.

Memories

First-rate advice for the first graduating class.

Professor Leon Ferraru, who taught Romance languages, would say in the classroom: "If you don't know the answer, don't shake your head from one side to the other because you'll mix up all your languages."

— Lillian Huriash Benowitz B'31
(shown above in her cap and gown)

Elegantly educated, with degrees from universities in France and a Ph.D. from Columbia University, Leon Ferraru joined Long Island University's original faculty to become a professor of romance languages, beloved as a scholar, a gentleman and especially, a gentle man.

From 1968 to 1990, artist Alfred Van Loen shared his love of metalworking, sculpting and media with art students on the C.W. Post Campus.

In one of the few such programs on the East Coast, marine science students at Southampton College regularly sail out to compare and contrast the material in their textbooks with the "real life" of the sea.

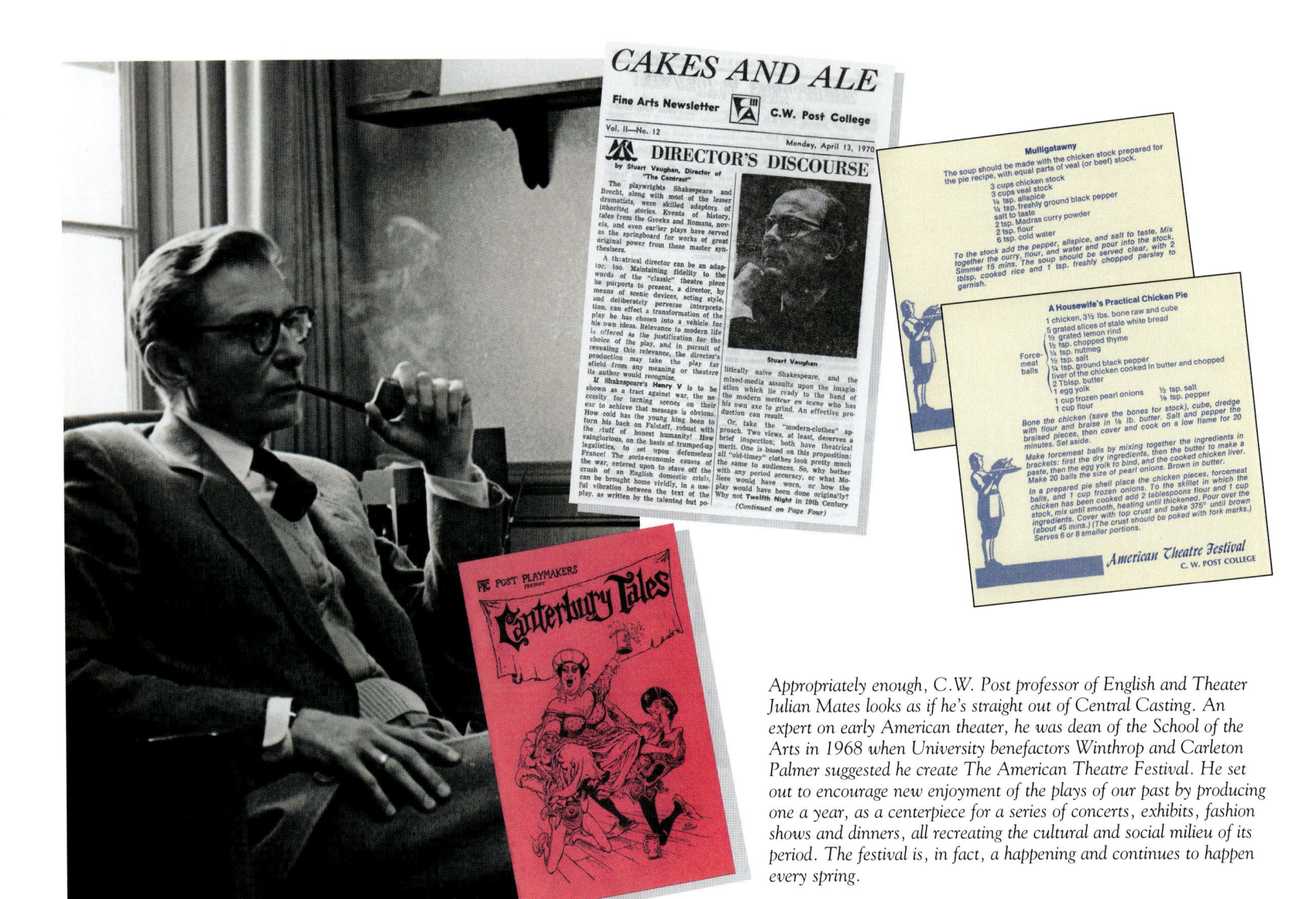

Appropriately enough, C.W. Post professor of English and Theater Julian Mates looks as if he's straight out of Central Casting. An expert on early American theater, he was dean of the School of the Arts in 1968 when University benefactors Winthrop and Carleton Palmer suggested he create The American Theatre Festival. He set out to encourage new enjoyment of the plays of our past by producing one a year, as a centerpiece for a series of concerts, exhibits, fashion shows and dinners, all recreating the cultural and social milieu of its period. The festival is, in fact, a happening and continues to happen every spring.

Southampton students of the '60s had particular affection for Bob Munford, an avuncular professor of art who became a campus favorite.

Long Island University has trained a large proportion of New York's school professionals. Shown is Professor Francis Roberts leading a Westbury School District group participating in a project based on the teachings of Yale's educational reformer, psychiatrist James Comer.

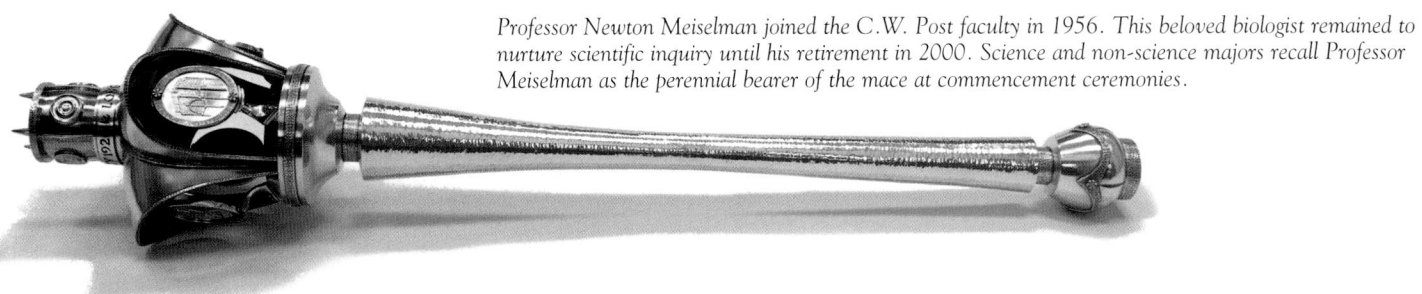

Professor Newton Meiselman joined the C.W. Post faculty in 1956. This beloved biologist remained to nurture scientific inquiry until his retirement in 2000. Science and non-science majors recall Professor Meiselman as the perennial bearer of the mace at commencement ceremonies.

Robert C. Whitford was a "great guy" in the eyes of Brooklyn Campus students of the '40s. A report in Seawanhaka, the Brooklyn Campus student newspaper, about his 1947 departure as head of the English department described the void he would leave, saying that he had the "most contact with the greatest number of students."

The Palmer School of Library and Information Science, founded in 1959 as the Graduate Library School, is nationally recognized for its American Library Association-accredited M.S. in Library and Information Science, and for its Ph.D. in Information Studies, the only program of its kind in the New York metropolitan area. Shown here is the evolution from card catalog to cutting-edge technology. Above: Professor Heting Chu.

Brooklyn's Arnold & Marie Schwartz College of Pharmacy and Health Sciences, originally established as the Brooklyn College of Pharmacy in 1886, has educated one fourth of the pharmacists in New York State.

A sound mind in a sound body. Legendary coach Rene Kern (left) inspired gymnasts on the Brooklyn Campus.

In the Fine Arts Center on the C.W. Post Campus, students paint a live model. Their demure inspiration is Edith Krum P'59.

PROFESSOR AT L.I.U. GOING STRONG AT 83

Dr. Walcott Gives Himself 2 More Years Before Retiring After 50 Years as Teacher

"Vigorous" is the word for Prof. Gregory Dexter Walcott, chairman of the Philosophy Department at Long Island University.

When the university began its twenty-sixth year last Thursday Dr. Walcott, by far the senior member of the faculty, began his twenty-fifth year on its staff.

Every one of the 6,000 alumni knows Dr. Walcott from having taken his "Philosophy 21," an orientation course required of all sophomores.

"I intend to go on teaching for two more years," Dr. Walcott said in his office at 385 Flatbush Avenue Extension, Brooklyn. "Then I shall be 85 years old and shall have completed fifty years as a college instructor. After that, I shall simply fade away."

The robust, round-faced, blue-eyed professor has given no evidence yet of fading away. In his classes, he stands up straight and pours forth the history of the human mind for an hour or two, without notes, in a resonant baritone. He runs down the stairs in the university building like a freshman. He works out frequently in the gymnasium to keep down his bulk, and has missed only one day from class because of illness since 1928.

Sees Standards Lowered

The standards of education have declined in the last fifty years, Dr. Walcott regretted to say. He could not tell exactly why, although higher costs of running a university undoubtedly had something to do with it.

"Of three to four million college graduates in this country, how many are outstanding intellectuals?" he asked. "Very few, I should say. Besides, regardless of university standards, how many Americans go to college? There are more college students than when I was an undergraduate, certainly, but the increase has not been what it should have been.

"And what do they study? Very few ever take a course in logic. They all study mathematics. Yet most men will require a knowledge of logic ten times for every occasion they need mathematics after they leave

Dr. Gregory D. Walcott — The New York Times

GOING STRONG: Dr. Gregory D. Walcott, 83, chairman of the Philosophy Department at Long Island University, who has been teaching forty-eight years and is still on job.

self. When he applied to enter Worcester Academy, Mass., at the age of 21, he had prepared himself sufficiently to start at the sophomore year.

He won every cash prize for scholarship the school offered and also worked in the laundry and dining room to maintain himself. When he was graduated he won a scholarship to Brown University. Graduating from Brown in 1897 at the head of his class, Dr. Walcott went to Union Theological Seminary again on a scholarship grant.

"I was acting preacher at several churches while a student," he said, "but I never was ordained. Although I had been brought up a Baptist, I just could not accept some things, like Christ raising Lazarus from the dead."

So Dr. Walcott turned to teaching. His first job was at Blackburn College, Carlinville, Ill., where he taught from 1904 to 1907.

"One of my students," he recalled, "was Helen Rebecca Steward, a freshman. She hated me then. In 1944 she married me. That was the only way

Gregory D. Walcott retired in 1954 after teaching for 50 years, 27 of them at Long Island University. Generations of Brooklyn students took his required Philosophy 21 class as sophomores. On his 83rd birthday, The New York Times said that "The Robust, round-faced, blue-eyed professor gives no evidence yet of fading away."

Serving as an inspiration well beyond the C.W. Post photography classroom, Arthur Leipzig welcomed students into his home, introduced them to contemporary greats of photography and took them on shoots throughout the metropolitan area. His influence was acknowledged in a recent exhibition of images by him and the many former students who are professional photographers. His works have been exhibited at museums and galleries in this country and abroad. Students will remember him as the professor who arrived every day on a scooter.

The School of Education at C.W. Post, focusing on child-centered education, has prepared thousands of teachers.

Many of the metropolitan area's speech, hearing and language therapists are Long Island University graduates. This tradition of excellence began in the '50s; it continues today as 21st century technology drives the programs at the Brooklyn and C.W. Post Campuses.

"There is no doubt ... that here in Brooklyn

a Long Island University could be established

which would do work second to none in the United States"

— Robert H. Roy, President,
University Club of Brooklyn,
quoted in the Brooklyn Eagle,
March 9, 1911

CHAPTER THREE
A HISTORY

STRUGGLE FOR ACCESS

by
Maren Lockwood Carden, Ph.D., Professor of Sociology, Brooklyn Campus
and
Susan E. Dinan, Ph.D., Assistant Professor of History, C.W. Post Campus

Long Island University's six campuses vary widely in look, function and tradition. But every graduate gets a degree from the same university, and despite the campuses' surface differences, every graduate benefits from the University's remarkable history of conviction and struggle.

The University's charter, awarded in 1926, expresses firm commitment to a special American place. The University was to be "located on Long Island ... and to operate on Long Island and in the City of Greater New York and vicinity."[1] From the Brooklyn end of the Island, where its first graduating class numbered only 92, the University expanded eastward after World War II to serve the rapidly-growing suburbs. By the mid-1960s it had added major campuses at C.W. Post, in Nassau County, and

The 1926 charter.

Southampton College, in eastern Suffolk County. Today students also attend regional campuses in Westchester, Rockland and Western Suffolk counties, over 70 off-campus extension sites, and the seven overseas centers of the Southampton-based Friends World Program.

This educational network each year awards about 2,000 bachelor's, 2,000 master's, and 50 doctoral degrees. Its nearly 30,000 undergraduate, graduate and non-credit students make it the eighth largest private university in the United States.

Over the years, students have benefited from the convenience of the University's geographical scope and from its unvarying commitment to universal education. The founders insisted that Long Island University be inclusive 60 years before the word "inclusive" entered the vocabulary of higher education.

They specifically named Jews and Catholics as beneficiaries of their determination to judge applicants by standards of scholarship alone. Soon, however, the University was known as a place where anyone could take advantage of its educational opportunities — women, members of any ethnic or racial group, those who were older or disabled or whose jobs created a need for evening and weekend classes. Today about one-third of students are African-American, one-eighth Hispanic and one-half white. About half the undergraduates are older than the traditional college student ages of 18-21 years. Although loyal alumni increasingly applaud their children's attendance, as at the beginning, many students are still the first in their families to attend college.

Long Island University students have consistently found programs geared to preparing them for the "outside world" with the depth and mental flexibility imparted by the liberal arts. Year after year, graduates leave to nourish the communities of the New York metropolitan area as medical, business, government, education, counseling and arts professionals.

Although it began with a distinctive mission, enthusiastic community support and powerful leaders, almost from the start Long Island University was buffeted by economic problems over which it had little control. The Depression diminished its enrollments and its sponsors' wealth. Before and during World War II, the draft drew away so many students it brought financial bankruptcy. Restored by the burgeoning enrollments enabled by the GI Bill, the University shrewdly anticipated suburban growth by purchasing a second campus in Nassau County, but community opposition (in what became known as the "Battle of Brookville") delayed the opening of the C.W. Post Campus for several years and deprived the University of tuition revenue.

By the early '60s, after campuses in Brentwood, Southampton, and at Mitchel Field were opened, the University was a major presence on Long Island — but the untimely death of President Richard Conolly in 1962 brought almost three years of irresolution, followed by a change of direction away from serving local Long Island and New York populations to an unsuccessful attempt at creating a national graduate research center on the C.W. Post Campus. It was to be partially funded by selling the Brooklyn Campus. That campus's passionate and effective opposition to the sale illustrated the kind of strength to be found within the University. Since then, the University has struggled to harness the energy of its widely separated campuses while encouraging them to maintain and develop the different identities upon which that energy depends.

The University has continued this struggle while weathering still other financial reverses. Yet even in the '70s and '80s, when the decline in enrollments throughout higher education hit particularly hard, the University coped. A

> *"The sociologist David Reisman told one faculty member that the colleges that were closing were not accustomed to adversity, whereas Long Island University had persevered through adversity again and again."*

1886
The Statue of Liberty is dedicated in New York Harbor.
The Brooklyn College of Pharmacy is established by the Kings County Pharmaceutical Society.

1887
Thomas Edison invents the record player.

1889
Jane Addams opens Hull House in Chicago, part of the settlement-house movement to help immigrant populations adjust to American life.

Non-University dates reprinted with permission from www.Historychannel.com. © A&E Television Networks. All rights reserved.

faculty member remembered that in 1979, one of the darker years, she asked the noted sociologist David Reisman, a Harvard specialist in higher education, whether the job she had been offered at the University would be secure. He urged her to take it, saying that most of the colleges that were closing were not accustomed to adversity, whereas Long Island University had persevered through adversity again and again. It would survive.

It did. The three main campuses today are as different as their geographical settings and histories. Brooklyn is frankly urban; its administration, faculty and students grapple with the problems of the city and embrace its myriad opportunities. C.W. Post, part of Long Island's "gold coast," is suburban with touches of old fashioned gentility; a majority of its students come from families that fled the city one or two generations ago to enjoy grass, air and a settled life undisturbed by the problems of poverty or the hoots and whistles of city life. Southampton College, in a setting where local business owners who would once have been farmers serve summer residents espousing the politics of Wall Street, is exurban: its campus has a small town closeness that combines for its students the settled life of suburbia with the renowned visual and literary arts of the community and the rigor of its own marine sciences specialties.

Creating an Open University in the 1920s

The Brooklyn residents who founded Long Island University in 1926 were part of a great national movement whereby local groups created local colleges to serve their communities. Since the later decades of the nineteenth century, colleges and college enrollments had been increasing rapidly as people responded to new industries' ever-increasing need for knowledge and knowledgeable people. Many different kinds of institutions were founded, including the great land grant colleges and universities authorized by the federal Morrill Acts of 1862 and 1890, state and municipal institutions, and private colleges. The publicly-funded institutions in particular were viewed as examples of democracy in action: they freed people to choose how to lead their lives and made vital contributions to the changing society's needs. It was perhaps fair that the businessmen who benefited so much from an educated work force should contribute heavily in the form of taxes. The hundreds of new private colleges responded to the same needs of students and society, but in their cases students paid for their education directly instead of having part of the cost borne by society through taxes. As befitted the times and the need for investment capital, most of these were offshoots of the Protestant denominations or, less commonly, the Catholic Church. A minority of them were non-denominational. Among these was Long Island University.

The University's founders belonged to the borough of Brooklyn. Once an independent city, Brooklyn had become part of New York in 1898. Its identity was formed during the nineteenth century when it was transformed from a series of rural villages and towns into an immense industrial and commercial city with docks, shipyards, warehouses and manufacturers. Successive waves of immigrants from Ireland, Germany, Italy, Russia and other countries provided the labor that enabled these businesses to prosper.

The business owners, often longtime Brooklyn residents with Protestant backgrounds, had founded Brooklyn's major cultural institutions — the Brooklyn Academy of Music, Prospect Park and the Brooklyn Museum — during the second half of the nineteenth century. In the early 1900s, they decided a university could bring together all of Brooklyn's educational and cultural institutions, providing an intellectual center and prestige for a borough that feared becoming an appendage to Manhattan. An early hope was to model Brooklyn's university after Columbia, consolidating existing teaching institutions like the Brooklyn Law School, the Long Island College Hospital, the Brooklyn College of Pharmacy, Adelphi College (then a women's college) and the Polytechnic Institute.[2] When these leaders applied to the New York State Board of Regents in 1913, however, the Regents agreed Brooklyn needed such an educational institution but rejected the plan because the would-be incorporators did not have enough financial support. (Much of the history of that period is recorded in an unpublished

> *"Jonas insisted that the University not discriminate."*

1891 — Needing a game to keep students busy between the baseball and football seasons, gym teacher James Naismith invents basketball in Springfield, Massachusetts.

1892 — The College of Pharmacy graduates its first class.

1898 — The five boroughs of New York are unified into a single city.

Ph.D. thesis written by Elliott S.M. Gatner, the Brooklyn Campus librarian, whose active involvement in University affairs gave him a broad view. See note 1.)

When more money became available in the 1920s, during the economic boom after World War I, Brooklyn's leaders revived the idea of a university, although with fewer components. By then, local demand was even greater. Brooklyn's population was to increase by 25 percent during the '20s, but as civic leaders, teachers and ministers pointed out, the only affordable places for its young people to get a liberal arts education were public — City College and Hunter College — and in Manhattan. Moreover, existing colleges and universities did not always welcome the immigrants who made up a large part of the borough's population.

Official permission came first for a public institution. In April 1926, the State authorized the Brooklyn branch of City University, which four years later became the separate institution of Brooklyn College. Almost daily, the Brooklyn Eagle reported on the activities of men determined to found a private university, and one of broader scope than a local college. On December 9, 1926, the paper noted that the New York State Board of Regents had granted Long Island University a provisional charter.

Most of the University's first trustees came from the same established Brooklyn families of Protestant background who had worked so hard to found it. However, newcomers were joining the old urban elite. The board's chairman, Ralph Jonas, who had worked to establish both the public and private institutions and had led the final push to get Long Island University's charter, was the son of a German Jewish immigrant. A successful attorney and banker, he often used his work in civic organizations and philanthropy to counter the discrimination that Jews suffered. For example, as a Jew he must have realized he would not have been able to buy one of the large, twelve-room houses built near the D subway line in central Brooklyn. Because Jonas insisted that the University not discriminate and because the other men on the board supported him, from the start Long Island University's students reflected the borough's and the city's diverse population.

Ralph Jonas, a successful Brooklyn attorney and businessman, spearheaded the establishment of Long Island University and was its first board chairman.

At the opening of the new institution, a local paper noted Brave University's triumph over the forces that kept Fair Education imprisoned.

Each with a Serious Purpose: The First 20 Years

Classes began in 1927, just before the nation's economic Depression, but by the time the University celebrated its first graduation in 1931 it had an enrollment of 1,575. The young

1901 Theodore Roosevelt becomes president at age 42.

1902 Record numbers of immigrants arrive, most from Italy, Austro-Hungary and Russia.

1903 The Wright brothers make their first flight at Kitty Hawk, North Carolina.

The College of Pharmacy moves to its first specially built home at 265-271 Nostrand Avenue in Brooklyn.

At its founding in 1926, Long Island University's mission was to educate the sons and daughters of the city's burgeoning immigrant population without regard to race, creed or national origin.

people who attended were typically children of immigrant eastern European Jews. Others came from Italy and western European countries. They lived at home and commuted to college by subway and streetcar. Some worked to pay their tuition. To accommodate them, even before the end of the '20s the University was offering courses in the late afternoons, evenings and in the summer.

Students majored in fields where they could find jobs, the men favoring business and accounting. Among the few women, popular majors included retail distribution studies or secretarial studies, through which a young woman might hope to find work in the wider world of Manhattan banks and insurance companies. Many would have preferred to train as teachers, but jobs in that field were scarce because of low turnover induced by the Depression. In 1929, the University formally affiliated itself with the long-established Brooklyn College of Pharmacy and thus added a popular new major.

Whatever their majors, students also took the liberal arts courses that had become standard at colleges across the United States. Indeed, it was state pressure to include liberal arts as well as technical courses that prompted Pharmacy to seek affiliation with the University.

As the Depression took hold, enrollment dropped below 900. Several of the University's founders were unable to provide the capital funds they had promised and the board could not find new donors. Additional money could not come from students, who already struggled to pay their modest fees. Budgets were cut.

Makeshift teaching arrangements, however, did not discourage students who already were accustomed to penny pinching. The University owned only one building, a former factory called University Hall, or more commonly, the "main building," at 300 Pearl Street (where the New York City Technical College now stands).[3] The biology lab was on Montague Street, lecture rooms were at 26 Court Street and gym and basketball classes were given at the Pacific Street 'Y.' Downtown had other attractions, too, according to a memoir prepared for a later reunion by Lillian Huriash Benowitz B'31. The men might "lose their way and wind up in the Star Burlesque or the Paramount Theater."[4]

College events reflected the formality of the times. The dean of women would invite female students and faculty to an "informal tea," to hear a talk on "Making a Business of Home Management" followed by the singing of college songs.[5] Not all the women were as decorous as this invitation implies: Dean George Robert Hardie noted that the "ladylike" matron in charge of the women's lounge "does her best to instill in women students good ideals and manners of conduct."[6] Graduation in 1931 showed students enjoying and struggling with contemporary sophistication. The student council held its commencement dance at the Hotel St. George. Benowitz recalled that the commencement luncheon, costing $1.75, took place at "the elegant Hotel Bassert" where "only those who had majored in French could understand the menu." At the Senior Ball some students worried over "the proper way to attack the soup" while others admired the "ravishing blondes of innumerable number."[7] Although its students were commuters to a campus of largely rented buildings, the University made sure its formal commencement was typical of those at more established institutions. Exercises were held at the Brooklyn Academy of Music, as they would be for many years to come.

> "The men might 'lose their way and wind up in the Star Burlesque or the Paramount Theater.'"

1904
Work begins on the Panama Canal. The first segment of the New York City subway opens.

1906
San Francisco earthquake.

1908
Henry Ford develops the Model T.

University Hall, the first building owned by Long Island University, was a converted factory at 300 Pearl Street where it used to join Tillary St.

Faculty member Leo Gershoy captured a spirit that prevailed for generations when he described the students of the 1930s. "Relations were close and friendly in the main, even affectionate on occasion.... A small minority was brilliant and brilliant mavericks: tough-minded, thoroughly pragmatic, and as self-sufficient mentally as they were self-supporting financially.... Many times they challenged me — on class procedures, on my facts and interpretations. I loved it, I must say — and this is not sentimental recollection, this is reality. And they loved it, too. They had intense loyalties, even to deep dislike of some of us and all-but-adoration for a few of us."[8] A student who exemplified this spirit in the 1950s was the late Rose Bird B'58, who eventually overcame a desperately poor background to become the first woman chief justice of the California Supreme Court.

Students, like faculty members and administrators, had a keen sense of their individual rights and social responsibilities. In 1936, the staff of what has become the University's longest running periodical, Seawanhaka, the student newspaper, tussled with the administration over censorship of the paper. In the later '30s and '40s the Campus was made aware of its few African-American students when one of them, Geraldo Guirty B'45, a member of the Seawanhaka staff, wrote passionately about discrimination in the nation and in the segregated military. He pointedly wondered how the University would respond if its basketball or football team encountered Jim Crowism.[9]

Guirty's answer began taking shape in 1936, when Coach Clair F. Bee was pressed by his predominantly Jewish, probably unbeatable, basketball team not to compete for places in Hitler's Berlin Olympics. He agreed. In later years he faced the exact situation Guirty described and refused to take his team to Kansas because his black and white athletes could not eat together or share the same accommodations.

(By unfortunate contrast, in the 1950s the University's sports brought it a different kind of prominence. A few of its basketball players, along with players from City College and elsewhere, succumbed to pressure from professional gamblers to "shave" points during games, triggering a scandal that forced the suspension of the team from intercollegiate basketball for several years.)

The generally young faculty members, like the students and the University administrators, worked very hard. They taught two, three and four subjects in the daytime and often wrote

Downtown Brooklyn extended itself in the early '30s, pushing Flatbush Avenue eastward past what became the University's present-day Brooklyn site.

1911 The Triangle Shirtwaist Factory fire kills 146 seamstresses, galvanizes the labor movement.

1913 Brooklyn leaders apply unsuccessfully to the New York State Board of Regents to charter a private university.

1914 World War I breaks out in Europe after the assasination of Archduke Ferdinand of Austria.

Controller, dean, and ultimately, president, Tristram Walker Metcalfe led the University through the 1930s and 1940s. Loved by students and faculty, he was as benevolent as he was firm.

1916 Margaret Sanger opens the first American birth control clinic, in Brooklyn.

1919 Dial telephones introduced.

1920 The 1920 census reveals that the U.S. population has surpassed 100 million and that the majority of Americans live in cities.
Prohibition goes into effect.

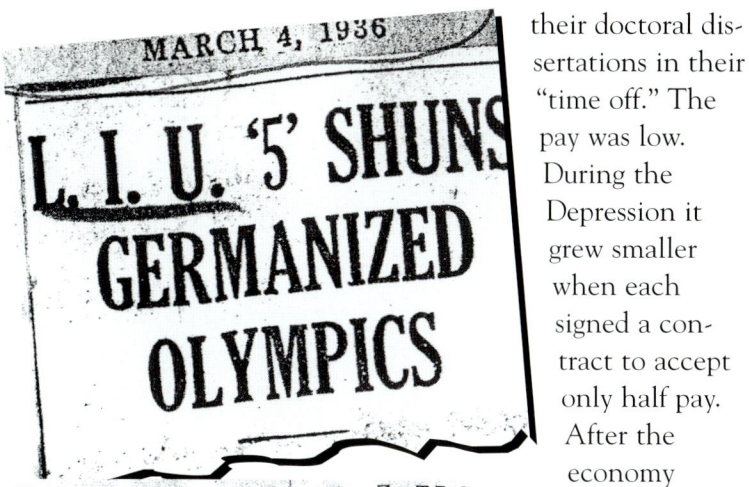

L. I. U. '5' SHUNS GERMANIZED OLYMPICS

Dean Metcalfe of L. I. U. Refuses to Let Basketball Team Join Nazi Olympics

By SOL LEVY

MARCH 4, 1936

The University's commitment to inclusiveness was carried out in the decisions of basketball Coach Clair F. Bee not to let his team compete for places in Hitler's 1936 Olympics or play in segregated states.

their doctoral dissertations in their "time off." The pay was low. During the Depression it grew smaller when each signed a contract to accept only half pay. After the economy recovered, a historian on the faculty recorded that the University repaid "every cent owed them."[10]

Though pressed for time and money, faculty members helped students take on the upper crust at its own games. One professor "actually formed what was then quintessentially English — a rugby team — and it not only played much tonier Ivy League campuses like Princeton and Yale but nurtured players like Bernie Kapatansky, who went on to play professional football."[11]

The man who assembled these faculty members and guided the University through the '30s and '40s was Tristram Walker Metcalfe. He led the University under the titles of controller, dean and, in 1942, president. Metcalfe embodied the qualities of his best students. Born and raised in Brooklyn, he had attended Public School 16, Boys High School and New York University. "A hard-nosed realist," he "ran the University as a benevolent despot." A former newspaperman whose specialty was education and who had been trained in accountancy, he knew every detail of the University's operations and was "stingy to a fault" with university money — but opened his personal checkbook to needy students.[12] When students faced the upheavals of conscription for military service in World War II, he let them complete a semester's classes early and arranged for accelerated degree programs.

Like many of its students in the service, the University faced dire threats during the war. Educating young people could only be accomplished with the tuition money they paid. During times of low enrollment, a long-established university with students from the most prosperous families in the nation could draw interest and even capital from millions of dollars of endowment. Hundreds of other colleges and community-focused young universities like Long Island University had no such financial cushion.

In 1941 when the military draft began, Long Island University's enrollment dropped by half and its income fell sharply. Fearing for their money, the banks that held its mortgages demanded payment. The University had either to sell all its holdings and close down or choose bankruptcy and fiscal reorganization under court supervision. In 1943, it chose the second course.

Metcalfe's reputation carried the University through. Judge Matthew T. Abruzzo, who presided over the University's financial affairs during the bankruptcy, commented later, "I had great respect for Mr. Metcalfe ... I felt that Brooklyn needed Long Island University and I had no intention of letting it die."[13] As Metcalfe had anticipated, the financial figures soon improved greatly. The government that had taken away students as GIs returned them as student veterans whose tuition, books and even some living costs were paid for under the GI Bill of Rights. Mary M. Lai B'42, H'86, today's treasurer and chief financial officer, helped enormously in speeding that recovery by organizing and even setting up the University's financial records, all by hand. She

During World War II, the halls and classrooms of Long Island University emptied, giving rise to the University's first great crisis.

1922 — James Joyce's "Ulysses," "The Wasteland" by T.S. Elliot, "Babbit" by Sinclair Lewis and "Siddhartha" by Hermann Hesse are published.

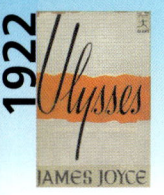

1923 — The Union of Soviet Socialist Republics is formed.

1924 — Robert Moses begins overseeing the building of at least 12 bridges and 35 highways in the New York City area.

> "The University had either to sell all its holdings and close down, or choose bankruptcy."

came to work for Long Island University in 1946 after an accidental subway meeting with a former professor led her to Metcalfe, who appointed her bursar. She worked "round the clock, seven days a week" until, 13 months later, she documented the University's solvency for the bankruptcy court. In 1947 the University, with all its debts paid, emerged from bankruptcy.

During and after the bankruptcy period, the veterans, who made up half the student body, were even more anxious than their predecessors had been to complete their educations. Professor Robert Spector of the English Department remembers speeding through his own undergraduate degree and, soon after, returning from graduate school to teach at "the most exciting place" where "students [were] desperate to learn." Some of his students were a little less desperate: Lloyd Newman B'52 remembered a few of them having a "couple of beers" before "we suddenly remembered our English class. We ran up to Dr. Spector's class trying to think of a good excuse, except he was glancing out of the window and could see us dashing out of the bar." Psychology Professor Murray Banks recognized another need. He organized inexpensive dances at nearby halls to give veterans a chance to meet local women. John L. Doria B'57 founded the LIU Jazz Club, contributing to veterans and non-veterans alike with a lengthy series of afternoon jazz programs.

The GI Bill did much more than turn around the University's finances; it also provided the impetus to expand eastward and open a campus in Nassau County to serve the needs of the veterans who had settled in the suburbs. By the later '40s extra funds were in hand. Metcalfe seized the opportunity to re-examine the founders' visions for the University. Some of these men would have wanted him to expand the Brooklyn base by developing graduate programs. Others, he thought, would have wanted him to focus on Long Island.

Metcalfe looked East. Long Island's population was increasing rapidly and the young families who moved out to its suburbs saw a college education as an integral part of their new way of life. On Sundays, Metcalfe took his family along and searched the large estates of Nassau County for a place suitable for the University's second campus. He regularly reported to the trustees on space for classrooms, costs of alterations, land for expansion, access roads and the character of surrounding neighborhoods. The trustees, however, reacted so cautiously that buying opportunities were being lost.

It is not clear why the trustees approached Metcalfe's proposed purchases so cautiously. Certainly, the new chairman of the board, William Zeckendorf, was no sluggard. He was a swashbuckling real estate developer in New York and Long Island who played a major role in scores of projects, including putting together the parcel of land on which the

With the post-war shift to suburbia, President Metcalfe cast his eyes eastward toward a new campus to serve the residents of the suburban communities that were sprouting on the potato fields of Long Island. Levittown (shown above) epitomized this trend.

© 1947 Newsday, Inc. Reprinted with permission.

1925
The Roaring '20s are in full swing.

1926
December 9
Provisional Charter (No. 3606) is granted to Long Island University by the New York State Board of Regents.

1927
June
Evening courses begin.

September
Classes begin: 312 students.

Charles Lindbergh lands in Paris, completing the first nonstop solo trans-Atlantic flight.
Babe Ruth hits a record 60 home runs in a season.

United Nations Building was constructed. Whatever the causes of the trustees' qualms, in May 1947 the University signed an agreement to purchase from the cereal heiress and entrepreneur Marjorie Merriweather Post the property that is now the C.W. Post Campus.

Metcalfe was just as diligent in his search for a permanent home for the University in Brooklyn. He personally checked buildings throughout the downtown area including many that Zeckendorf identified as having future potential. He did not want a repetition of the problems of Pearl Street, a neighborhood "so run-down that our evening enrollment was always small and the registration of women was low." His reports to the board were blunt: one building not only had inconvenient subways, but "borders upon the Navy Yard … district and the lower Hicks Street house of disrepute."[14]

Eventually, in 1950, the University bought the Brooklyn Paramount Theater building and the adjacent offices now known as the Metcalfe building. Because it rented out the Theater until 1962, Brooklyn residents could still watch films and later attend "rock 'n' roll" concerts at the Paramount where Allan Freed and others served as masters of ceremony. Long Island University's home was in the office space above and next door to the Theater.

President Metcalfe died in 1952, soon after he had shepherded these defining purchases through the board of trustees. His last commencement speech, read in his absence, expressed the idealism and certainties of the era. "[D]edicate yourselves to helping your country demonstrate to all nations that democracy works better in practice than any other form of government." The students that year were confident that their American way of life was the best — and so it seemed to their successors through the '50s and half of the '60s.

On the campus, faculty, staff, administrators and students settled into the newly-acquired buildings and continued to build community out of the ever-increasing diversity of their colors, ethnicity, qualifications, interests and backgrounds. Blacks had started to move to Brooklyn from Manhattan, the South and the Caribbean. In 1960, eight years after Metcalfe's death, they formed 12 percent of the borough's population, with a far smaller percentage of Puerto Ricans. The first African-American faculty member, Richard P. Grossley, had been hired in 1947, but until the mid-'60s, nearly all faculty members were white. Many had earned their doctorates at graduate schools in New York and their lives focused on the city. For faculty and students alike, Long Island University was a kind of neighborhood in the city of neighborhoods. Close quarters encouraged informal contacts, and faculty, staff and students discussed their work, exchanged gossip and explored ideas until people came to know and care for one another.

The Brooklyn Paramount Theater was eventually converted into the Brooklyn Campus Metcalfe building.

1928 The Brooklyn College of Pharmacy affiliates with Long Island University.

1929 The Brooklyn College of Pharmacy moves to 600 Lafayette Avenue. The University acquires 300 Pearl Street. The stock market crashes.

1930 The Society of the Optimates (honor society) is started by Philosophy Professor Gregory Walcott.

Advocate for Health: Affiliation with the Brooklyn College of Pharmacy

One important segment of the University, the Brooklyn College of Pharmacy, was based at 600 Lafayette Avenue, about a quarter of a mile from the Brooklyn Campus. The College is proud to predate by almost 40 years the University of which it is now a part. In the later 1870s, Dr. Edward Robinson Squibb, whose Brooklyn-based pharmaceutical company, E. R. Squibb and Sons, would become nationally known, was leading a national battle to improve the quality of pharmaceuticals that would result in the federal Pure Food and Drug Act of 1906. One part of that contest, which in Brooklyn was taken on by the Kings County Pharmaceutical Society, was to overcome "the incompetence, not to mention the unethical practices, of both retail and wholesale pharmacists in the 1880s" by providing a specific training program.[15] On April 22, 1886, the Society received a charter for the Brooklyn College of Pharmacy. The College was ahead of its time: it began training pharmacists well before 1904, the date that New York State required pharmacists to have two years of college before they could practice.

When the College opened in 1891, its home in a Brooklyn parlor (for a lecture hall) and kitchen (for a laboratory) reflected the state of some of the best pharmaceutical training of the time. Its subsequent moves to progressively larger and more elaborate quarters reflect the profession's development and growth. A move to 600 Lafayette Avenue came one year after its affiliation with Long Island University. The affiliation enabled what was now the Brooklyn College of Pharmacy at Long Island University to meet new state educational requirements and left Pharmacy with considerable autonomy. It retained its board of trustees, whose members controlled all instruction, elected its chief officer, the dean of Pharmacy, with the approval of the University's president, and controlled its budget.

Pharmacy students' lives revolved around their five-story collegiate Gothic laboratory and classroom building. Their isolation contributed to the strong sense of community that had always been characteristic of the College. Except for the institutional title

In 1928, the Brooklyn College of Pharmacy became affiliated with the University. An important New York educational resource, the College traces its roots to 1886. The graduating class of 1892 is shown in front of the original building, which was replaced in 1929 with a facility that was used for the next six decades.

on their diplomas, they had almost no contact with the University. All their professors were from Pharmacy and all their classes were held in the new building. All shared the experience of Professor Chester Reiss's classes when he "dragged these druggists" through Shakespeare and much more of English and American literature, and when he directed their annual musical production. Their own formidable team competed in the Pharmacy Basketball League; among its members was Howard Sternheim B'54, founder of Brooklyn's Thriftway Drug. Their fifth floor basketball court, reputed to be the best in the city, was for years home of the LIU Blackbirds.

During the next three decades, as knowledge in the field of pharmacy burgeoned students needed even more training. In 1957, the College introduced an M.S. in Pharmacy Administration that also drew on the larger University's resources: it included 15 hours of work in business administration. A few years later, the school extended the

---

1931
First Long Island University commencement.
Tristram Walker Metcalfe appointed comptroller.
Clair Bee appointed director of athletics.

1932
Depression forces 50% cut in faculty paychecks.

1933
Adolf Hitler becomes chancellor of Germany.
Prohibition ends in the United States.
Tristram Walker Metcalfe is appointed dean of the University.

B.S. program from four to five years so students could specialize in retail, hospital or industrial pharmacy.

The school remained very close to the Brooklyn community. As it does now, it trained at least a fourth of the New York City area's (and, indeed, New York State's) pharmacists. Imbued with a sense of civic responsibility, it continued to pressure for new laws that would improve the profession. For the borough and the city, it created what eventually became the Arnold & Marie Schwartz Drug Information Center, a telephone information service for pharmacists, physicians and manufacturers. The extensive collection of drug information on which the service drew formed the basis for a Washington, D.C.-based national Mediphone service. In 1959, the College built the first radioisotope laboratory in New York State. It also initiated a M.S. in Drug Regulatory Affairs, the first such academic program in the world. As it does today, it sponsored a variety of seminars, symposia and annual public health forums.

Post-War Suburbia: Founding C.W. Post in the 1950s and 1960s

Many of the people who moved from the city to the Long Island suburbs along the highways built by the legendary Robert Moses were war veterans who bought their houses with federally-funded, interest-free loans. Like other people who had moved to the Island, these men and their family members were anxious to attend college. An earlier phase of suburban growth in the 1920s and 1930s had led to Adelphi University's move from Brooklyn in 1929 and to the foundation of Hofstra University in 1935. Long Island University led a second wave. During the 1950s and 1960s it would be joined by Dowling College (formerly a branch of Adelphi), two branches of the New York Institute of Technology, a branch of Polytechnic University and SUNY at Stony Brook. The rapid development of new campuses proved just how necessary they were to life in the suburbs.

Although the trustees agreed to purchase the Post estate in 1947, the actual sale did not go through immediately, and even after that it was eight years before teaching started.

Some residents of this exclusive section of Nassau County — the so-called Gold Coast made famous by F. Scott Fitzgerald's "The Great Gatsby" — put up tremendous resistance to a university campus, fearing it would bring undesirables (in boisterousness, race, or ethnicity) and lower property values. In legal proceedings, they argued implausibly but effectively that Brookville zoning laws permitted schools but not a university. Eventually, in October 1951, the University was granted a zoning variance and, confident of eventual success, continued offering the evening extension courses it had started a few years before using classrooms in Hicksville and Oyster Bay high schools.

Further delays arose when the State Education Department, which previously had supported the University's plans, raised new questions. It wrote that most local veterans had either used up their college benefits or forfeited them, that other men who might have planned to attend the college were being drafted for the Korean War, that students would go to the campuses of the new State University system, and that Long Island University's academic organization was not keeping pace with its physical development. It seemed

Community anxieties delayed the opening of the C.W. Post Campus for eight years, but once students arrived, they frequently lived up to the area's stately heritage.

1935
The Social Security Act becomes law.

1936
Dean Metcalfe of L. I. U. Refuses to Let Basketball Team Join Nazi Olympics
Long Island University's unbeaten basketball team refuses to compete with other U.S. teams for a place in Olympic games being held in Nazi Germany.

1938
German Nazis attack Jews and their property during Kristallnacht.

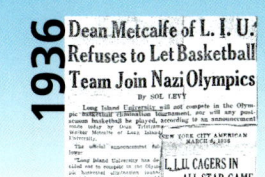

that the Nassau County campus of Long Island University might have missed the opportunity to establish itself.

The decisive action needed to bring the Brookville campus into being was finally taken by President Metcalfe's successor, Admiral Richard Lansing Conolly, who was appointed in November 1953, almost two years after Metcalfe's death. An Annapolis graduate with a master's from Columbia, Conolly's final assignment as a four-star admiral had been as President of the Naval War College. "Close-in" Conolly was a no-nonsense 'full steam ahead and damn the torpedoes' type of naval officer."[16] Moving with his wife into an apartment in the Southern Wing of the Post estate house, he courted the local landowners, promising them the Brookville campus would have none of the hustle and bustle of the University's urban campus in Brooklyn. Finally, in September 1955, after he had directed a summer's worth of building, renovating and fast-paced administrative reorganization, the college triumphantly opened to its first class of 102 male and 19 female full-time students. At an assembly three months later, these students heard Conolly announce that the University had received accreditation for the campus from the Middle States Association of Colleges and Secondary Schools.

In keeping with Metcalfe's decision to move the University out to the people of Long Island, the trustees had conceived of the Brookville campus as a branch of the main campus in Brooklyn, perhaps with a name like Long Island University, Brookville. The board ultimately revised this decision, probably at Conolly's urging, and gave the new campus a separate identity. By naming it C.W. Post College, after Marjorie Merriweather Post's father, the breakfast cereal pioneer, they sought to flatter his daughter (in the vain hopes of receiving from her a large endowment) and to gloss over the Brooklyn roots that bothered the local residents.

Charles William Post had been an advocate of a non-stimulating vegetarian diet to which he contributed the coffee substitute Postum and the cereals Grapenuts and Post Toasties (originally named Elijah Manna). On October 29, 1954, the hundredth anniversary of his birth, C.W. Post College was formally dedicated and Marjorie Merriweather Post unveiled her father's portrait in the Great Hall of the mansion. Marjorie, born in 1887, was an only child. Her father raised her as the son he never had, so she hunted, fished and tagged along on C.W.'s factory visits and business trips. She was well prepared to take over the family business, valued at over $20 million in 1914. (At the time of her death in 1973, the company was worth $200 million.) Her husbands were as financially successful as she; among them were the financial tycoon E.F. Hutton and Joseph Davies, Franklin Roosevelt's ambassador to the USSR.

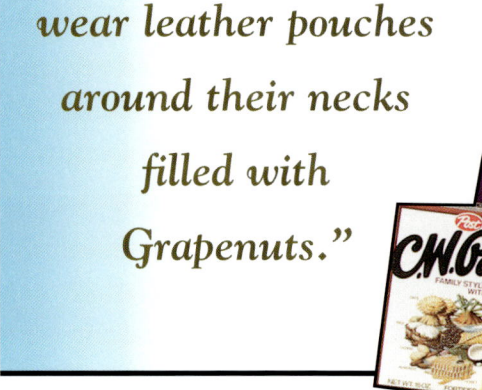

"Freshmen had to wear leather pouches around their necks filled with Grapenuts."

Faculty, students and staff used every inch of this main building and its outbuildings to teach, study and work. Classes met in the mansion, which became the Administration Building, and in a smaller residence built for Mrs. Post's daughter (College Hall). The guest house became the library and within a couple of years, barns and stables became classrooms and laboratories. (Professor Newton Meiselman recalled that although the animals were gone, the flies remained.) The caretaker was Sylvester Cangero, one of the Italian immigrants who made up Mrs. Post's grounds staff.

Meanwhile, Conolly launched an enormous building initiative that included a dining hall, two dormitories and a heating plant. To please local residents, architects designed the buildings in Colonial and Georgian styles. Room and board in the dormitories was $815 per year, with two men sharing each room. (The College added a woman's dormitory the following year). In 1960-1961, the College constructed additional residence halls for women and men, as well as a biology building, language lab and library. In 1961, Conolly dedicated the Little Theater, finally giving Post's dynamic theater community a home. The College built more dormitories, but in the fall of 1962, because of construction delays, juniors and seniors who were promised rooms in the new lodges wound up in hotels. Students appreciated a month or

1939 Clair Bee's Blackbirds win their first National Invitational Tournament.

1940 Winston Churchill becomes Britain's Prime Minister.

1941 On December 7, Japan attacks Pearl Harbor. University offers courses for prospective Flying Cadets.

two of maid service, private telephones and television sets, but the commute and the lack of closet space made them anxious to move on campus.

Post students tended to major in the same kinds of practical subjects as their Brooklyn counterparts. As at Brooklyn, all students took basic liberal arts courses, but in contrast had a more flexible curriculum organized around divisions instead of departments. Pre-professional programs in education and business administration were popular. After 1959, more advanced students could work for M.A. degrees in education, and within a few more years they would be able to specialize in business administration at the Arthur T. Roth Graduate School of Business Administration, now the College of Management, and in library science at what was to become the Graduate Library School, now the Palmer School of Library and Information Science. Since most graduate and many undergraduate courses were offered in the evening, Post soon became a place where people who worked in New York City or on Long Island could attend college near their homes.

Student life for these commuting graduate students was very different from that of the residential students. Like college students throughout the U.S., the residents knew an era of fraternities and sororities, pep rallies and sporting events. In 1955, the Women's League sponsored the first formal dance, the Blue Christmas Ball, which became an annual tradition. The Fathers' Club honored athletic teams at sports dinners and at one time offered emergency loans to needy students. For part of their first semester, freshmen wore dinks (little green hats) and nametags, and were required to attend all campus lectures and football games. At one time, they had to carry two box tops from any Post cereal and wear leather pouches around their necks filled with Grapenuts. Upperclassmen auctioned off freshmen with large numbers of infractions as 24-hour "slaves." "Hazing," said the Pioneer, Post's student newspaper, gave freshmen a crash course on

Charles William Post and daughter Marjorie Merriweather Post, circa 1888. (photo: Hillwood Museum, Washington, D.C.)

their college that would enable them to better enjoy the college experience.

Every place on campus had its own rules, often of the "Thou shalt not" variety. Students could not talk in the library, enter classes after the hour or remove food from the dining hall. Rules proliferated especially in women's dormitories. Women could not wear slacks or Bermuda shorts except inside the dormitory before 6 p.m. and on the way to the tennis courts or the riding stables. If a "girl" appeared wearing sneakers in the dining hall, or curlers anywhere, she received three demerits from the dormitory monitor. Rules forbade men from venturing beyond the first floor lounge of the women's residence halls. A man met his date there under the scrutiny of other women residents and returned her by the curfew.

The vigorous social life did not eclipse the college's intellectual activity. In the early 1960s, C.W. Post Dean and Professor Eugene Arden created the campus's honors program, over objections of elitism voiced by a professor of education who also coached the football team. The program proved very successful and grew dramatically; never again did it face charges of snobbery. The wealth of some members of the Long Island social elite who lived locally also benefited college intellectual life. Carleton Palmer, a generous donor to C.W. Post, underwrote the literary magazine Confrontation in 1968. His wife Winthrop, took the lead in its creation: under editor Martin Tucker it has completed more than thirty distinguished years of publication.

The Campus's dynamic academic environment was in part due to its diverse faculty. Among the professors in the early years was Stefan Wolpe, an acclaimed avant-garde composer who led the music department. Wolpe composed for orchestras including the Berlin Philharmonic, regularly toured to lecture on modern classical music and engaged actively in the Post community. He conducted the Post college band that performed bi-weekly concerts, organized

1942
William Zeckendorf Sr. is elected president of the Board of Trustees.
Dean Tristram Walker Metcalfe is elected first president of Long Island University.

1943
Lowest enrollment: 307.
The University elects to seek bankruptcy protection.

1944
Congress passes the GI Bill of Rights, which will finance college educations and home bank mortgages for many World War II veterans.

symphonic bands to play at football games and regularly lectured on campus. As well as composing the music to the college's song, "Alma Mater," the lyrics to which were written by English Professor Julian Mates, he composed the musical score to Moliere's "Adventures of Scapin" when the Post Playmakers theater group staged the play in 1960.

Elaborating the Network

President Conolly knew that the Post and Brooklyn campuses were too far apart to serve all interested students on Long Island. He identified other geographical areas to serve and, at the same time, other educational specialties to develop.[17] His work was facilitated by Board Chairman Zeckendorf, by then a major developer in Nassau County. To enable working people to take courses in the evenings and weekends at places close to their homes, the University created a number of extension programs. One has grown into the University's Brentwood Campus, which today has almost 700 graduate and upper division students. Another program, formalized in 1957, two years before Brentwood, was located at Mitchel Air Force Base in Hempstead. The military authorities responded enthusiastically to retired Admiral Conolly's proposal that Long Island University establish the first private, degree-granting institution situated on a U.S. military installation: in the post-Sputnik era of keeping up with Soviet science, the federal government encouraged higher education for the military. The men themselves welcomed the opportunity to take college courses during their off-duty hours and the chance to complete the greater part of a degree during the normal tour of duty of two to three years. Soon Mitchel College had two major and three minor satellites located between Governors Island in the west and Montauk in the east. Although the base closed in 1961 and the last remnant of the college in 1967, several satellite programs remained until the last one, at Fort Hamilton in Brooklyn, closed in the 1980s.

Conolly made careful decisions about how to expand. For example, he rejected a College of Engineering. The trustees previously had turned down a proposal presented by Zeckendorf for a College of Engineering at Woodmere on property to be donated by Mrs. William Fox, but the Board then asked Conolly to consider developing engineering courses at Post. Conolly again studied the University's actual and potential student body and decided against the idea. Long Island had too few students with appropriate mathematical and scientific training who wanted to take engineering courses. Furthermore, the engineering schools in New York State already had plenty of spaces for students. (The board briefly revived the idea after Conolly's death and a School of Engineering became part of the plans of a later successor, R. Gordon Hoxie.)

Conolly understood the needs of the people on Long Island. Within a few years of his arrival he abandoned the idea of making C.W. Post a small, elite liberal arts college and encouraged it to expand into a college for any committed and qualified student. He provided these students with practical, career-oriented programs that contributed to their lives and to the larger life of the nearby communities where they lived. Brentwood, Mitchel College and the extension programs served similar students in similar ways, as did Brooklyn. And all these students, from Kings County in the west to Suffolk County in the east, could attend college at hours suited to their needs by taking day, weekend, evening and summer courses.

As a result of its expansion across Long Island, the University grew substantially. In 1955, the total enrollment was approaching 3,000. Ten years later, it was approaching 13,000, with about half at Post and half at Brooklyn.

Just as he carefully planned for the University's growth, so Conolly planned for his own succession. He was contemplating retirement and had begun identifying possible successors for the trustees to consider when, in March 1962, he and his wife died in a plane crash at what was then Idlewild Airport.

> "In 1955, the University's enrollment was approaching 3,000. Ten years later, it was approaching 13,000."

1945 
World War II ends.

1946 
Mary Lai appointed bursar.
Record-breaking enrollment: 2,879.
The Long Island University Band, led by Professor Raymond Shannon, plays at a Brooklyn Borough Hall celebration for Brooklyn Dodgers.

1947 
Jackie Robinson becomes the first black player in baseball's Major Leagues.
The University agrees to purchase Marjorie Merriweather Post's estate in Brookville, Long Island.

Arts and Marine Sciences in Southampton

The trustees appointed one of their own members, John H. G. Pell, a Harvard graduate, to succeed Conolly. During Pell's two-and-a-half year administration, the last major piece of Long Island University was put in place: Southampton College.

Like the Brooklyn Campus, Southampton was the product of a community-based movement for a local educational institution. In 1961, after twenty years of informal activism, residents of eastern Suffolk County, including local merchants who saw the advantage of more year round residents, founded the College Committee of Eastern Long Island to campaign for a local liberal arts college. Conolly's death meant that almost all of their negotiations were with the interim Chancellor. Pell was a descendant of the Westchester Pells who gave their name to the town of Pelham. An investor, he owned and had developed the upstate New York tourist attraction Fort Ticonderoga. The proposed college certainly fit into the University's plans for a Long Island network of colleges, but the board members' experience with local opposition in Brookville made them cautious. To be quite sure the Southampton community would support the college, the trustees insisted that the Committee offer convincing documentation and conducted their own survey on the same point. They also studied demographic data on the expanding population of Suffolk County. The 1960 census showed that between 1950 and 1960 the number of 15 to 24 year olds had more than doubled, to 65,000. Demographers predicted several more decades of rapid growth. The University agreed with Southampton's College Committee that it should expand eastward once again.

Pell let the Southampton community know the University could not afford to found a college in Southampton unless local residents purchased a site on its behalf. The College Committee began searching for a site and raising the funds to acquire it. In 1962, local advocates bought the Tucker Mill Inn, a windmill-dominated property in the Shinnecock Hills that originally had been a private estate. In the same year, the trustees approved the creation of Southampton College of Long Island University. The first class of 250 freshmen enrolled in fall 1963. A majority of these students came from Nassau County, which the University had not included in its population survey, creating a larger-than-expected need for residential facilities. As a small college, Southampton was not immediately able to fund the extensive professional programs offered at the much larger Post and Brooklyn Campuses. Instead, it concentrated on developing the liberal arts. By the late '60s the administration and faculty, under the leadership of Provost Edward C. Glanz, focused particular attention on the marine sciences and the creative arts — fields in which the students were especially interested and which took advantage of the location of the campus near the Atlantic Ocean and Long Island Sound and of the Hamptons' growth as a haven for artists.

The fine arts formed a critical link between college and community when the College and the local Parrish Art Museum worked together to sponsor lectures and art exhibitions. In April, 1964, the College began hosting an annual Festival of the Arts whose importance was evident when local artists of the caliber of Willem de Kooning arrived to open it.

Today, Southampton College's marine science program is nationally renowned. Its founders in the 1960s took advantage of ideal natural laboratories in nearby Shinnecock Bay, the ocean, and in

> "Willem de Kooning opened the Festival of Arts."

In contrast to the "Battle of Brookville," East End leaders actively solicited a college for their community. Here, a brochure they prepared.

1948 — Basketball coach Clair Bee refuses to enter the team in a Kansas City tournament because of Jim Crow restrictions on accomodations.

1949 — The first annual George Polk Awards for journalism are awarded in memory of journalist George Polk.

1950 — The University purchases the Brooklyn Paramount Theater and an adjoining 11-story office building at 385 Flatbush Avenue Extension.
Graduate courses begin in Brooklyn for master of arts and master of science degree programs.
North Korea invades South Korea, sparking the Korean War.

the surrounding salt ponds, tidal creeks, dunes and salt marshes. As the years passed and the field developed the College was to develop specialties in the biology, chemistry and vertebratology of the sea as well as in oceanography.

Academic and community programs were only part of the identity of the College. Students were forging the rest. In the school's very first year, for example, they formed a fire brigade that for years helped in local emergencies. Fraternities and sororities became popular, and in 1965, Sigma Lambda Chi kicked off its annual all-campus Carnation Ball. Enrollment increased impressively and by the College's second year there were over 600 students, including 200 upper division transfer students who wanted the small college experience Southampton offered. In June 1967, 131 seniors celebrated the College's first commencement. One graduate, Armand LaMaccia, would return to the College to teach in the Psychology Department, while his classmate Andrew Stein would become Manhattan Borough President.

With the creation of Southampton College under Chancellor Pell, Long Island University had residential campuses at each end and the middle of the Island. It was that middle where Pell's successor, R. Gordon Hoxie, would focus his attention.

The Controversial Ambitions of R. Gordon Hoxie: 1964-1968

In 1964, the board appointed R. Gordon Hoxie to head the University under the new title of chancellor. An historian, he was thoroughly at home in the

S'hampton College Opens First Year With Student Body of 244

Local history was made Monday morning when Southampton College opened its doors for its inaugural year. A branch of Long Island University, the local college is the only four-year, liberal arts college in Eastern Suffolk County.

For its inaugural year, Southampton College has a freshman class of 244 students, far in excess of the 150 students originally estimated as the maximum a new college in this area could attract in its first year. Of this student body, 165 are dormitory students living on campus and 79 are commuting students. The latter figure includes 28 student nurses who are freshmen at the Suffolk School of

Southampton Press September 26, 1963.

In the early days of Southampton College, as at all the campuses during their formative years, students developed extraordinary feelings of pioneering pride.

University, having been dean of the Brooklyn Campus and more recently dean of the C.W. Post Campus. With a stocky figure and an imposing voice, he was already a well-known figure both on campus and among the estate-holding residents of Brookville, for whom he and his wife gave splendid versions of the dinner parties that were typical of the '60s. (The next day his wife would carry a great bowl of flowers from their home to Hoxie's office.) He projected energy, enthusiasm and vision.

Hoxie immediately put aside Metcalfe's and Conolly's conception of the University as a network of local institutions serving the whole of Long Island and replaced it with a vision entertained long before by a few of the University's founders — making it a nationally-recognized graduate university. Its center was to be on land adjacent to that occupied by the buildings of C.W. Post. There Hoxie planned a graduate campus with a full-scale graduate liberal arts program and dormitories for students and their families. Nearby would be a Law Center. Thirty miles away, adjacent to the Brookhaven National Laboratory, would be a graduate Institute of Science and Engineering. The University would attract doctoral students from across the country.

In keeping with his ambitions, Hoxie moved the University's Administration Center from its old home in Brooklyn to a small but stately mansion next to C.W. Post. The Center's physical separation from C.W. Post as well as Brooklyn symbolized not only his dislike of Brooklyn, but also his disinterest in the University's undergraduate programs. He left the provosts of the C.W. Post and Brooklyn Campuses to administer those, and placed all

---

1951
Basketball players from Long Island University (and other campuses) are caught shaving points for gamblers, forcing the suspension of the team from intercollegiate competition.

The University closes the purchase of the estate of Marjorie Merriweather Post in Brookville, Long Island.

1952
Ralph Ellison publishes "Invisible Man"; Ernest Hemingway publishes "The Old Man and the Sea."

President Tristram Walker Metcalfe dies.

1953 
Admiral Richard L. Conolly is named president of University.

Francis Crick and James Watson discover the "double helix" of DNA.

graduate programs in the hands of university-wide administrators directly responsible to him. These included two graduate programs he had built up before becoming chancellor: the Arthur T. Roth Graduate School of Business Administration and the Carleton and Winthrop Palmer Library School — both named after their building's donors. No graduate programs existed at Southampton College. In his vision not only would it remain an undergraduate institution, but it had to "plan on a self-help 'boot-strap' operation" to decrease its financial dependence on its institutional parent.[18]

Southampton was young and small and could say little about its reduced role in the University. C.W. Post's future was so unclear that it, too, said little. Brooklyn's faculty, administration and students, however, were completely unwilling to become an appendage of the University Center. They believed their mission was to respond to the urban struggles of the 1960s.

During the 1950s, most American cities saw middle class residents depart in their newly acquired cars along new highways to new suburbs. Places like Long Island flourished. Places like Brooklyn declined. The borough became increasingly working class and poor. Many people perceived its problems as racial, but they were in fact economic. The minority population was still small. In 1957, blacks made up 12 percent and Puerto Ricans six percent of the otherwise white population. With industry moving out, the mostly-white Brooklyn residents could not find the well-paying jobs in industry that had supported previous generations. The borough's 15 breweries closed, unable to compete with larger firms out west. The Brooklyn Eagle, one symbol of the borough, stopped publishing in 1955. The Brooklyn Dodgers, a second symbol, left in 1957 for a more accessible stadium, larger and more prosperous crowds, and greatly increased profits. In 1966, the Navy decommissioned the Brooklyn Navy Yard, once by far the largest employer in the borough. Most people believed that Brooklyn was in serious decline.

The 1967 proposal of Chancellor R. Gordon Hoxie (above) to sell the Brooklyn Campus and centralize the University in Nassau County led to one of the most controversial eras in the University's history.

The Brooklyn provost, William M. Birenbaum, was one of the few who saw hope for the city, and in particular for Brooklyn. He believed the Brooklyn Center, as it was then known, should embrace the city's problems and retain its historic mission. It should boost young people — from Manhattan as well as Brooklyn — into jobs and enrich their lives.

Moreover, he wanted the campus to stay involved in the social problems and cultural activities of the city and the world. An Urban Affairs Conference initiated by students in 1963 was repeated annually for seven years. Each attracted many student representatives from far-away U.S. colleges including men and women from historically black institutions. Political science Professor Leo Pfeffer, who had argued before the U.S. Supreme Court on Church/State and civil rights issues, organized a Bill of Rights Conference whose speakers included members of the U. S. and New York State supreme courts. A lecture series commemorated the twentieth anniversary of the founding of the United Nations. An International Writers Conference organized by Professors Robert Spector and Martin Tucker attracted 37 writers from five continents, many of whose works have become classics. Each year during the spring break, Professor Harry Stucke took members of the business school

> *"The Brooklyn provost was one of the few who saw hope for the city and for Brooklyn."*

1954
An Extension (later, College) is established at Mitchel Air Force Base.
C.W. Post College is dedicated in a Great Hall ceremony.

1955
C.W. Post classes begin with 102 men, 19 women, and eight faculty members.

1956
The Montgomery, Alabama bus boycott is organized by Martin Luther King Jr.

management club on a tour of northeast industrial plants including steel mills, breweries and glass manufacturers.

Even though President Hoxie was preoccupied with plans for the graduate campus out in Brookville, some new buildings went up in Brooklyn. As with similar ones at Post and Southampton, their financing was arranged by Mary Lai.

She took advantage of low-cost loans from the federal government's Department of Housing and Urban Development and, later, from the Department of Health Education and Welfare and from New York State loans and grants authorized by the Higher Education Acts of 1963 and 1965. Funds from these sources were used at Brooklyn to build the 16-story dormitory that in those days included faculty apartments. Birenbaum encouraged the faculty to live there and in the University-owned commercial apartment building on adjacent Willoughby Street. Faculty members enjoyed the convenient location, inexpensive rents and views of the Brooklyn and the Manhattan bridges even though the immediate neighborhood was severely depressed. By the end of the '60s the University had squeezed in parking spaces, tennis courts and a soccer field.

Birenbaum's vision of an independent, socially involved, urban campus led in his informal, personal style did not mesh with Hoxie's vision of a suburban-based, nationally-recognized university led by a chancellor occupied with grand expansion plans. Their ideas and personalities clashed repeatedly. Eventually, in March, 1967, Hoxie demanded Birenbaum's resignation. Birenbaum was so close to the students and faculty that over half of them immediately rose in his support.

At a time when large demonstrations had occurred at only at a few radicalized universities like Berkeley, 1,500 chanting, sign-carrying students prevented Hoxie from reaching the office he still kept in Brooklyn. Over 90 percent of the students boycotted classes, and the faculty, as concerned as the students, voted overwhelmingly that it had "no confidence" in Hoxie. The students at Southampton College, also feeling left out of Hoxie's plans and still lacking basic facilities, expressed their support of Brooklyn in a one-day strike.

Eventually the protests ended, but Hoxie had forced Birenbaum to leave.

Within a few months of Birenbaum's departure an even more serious problem arose. Rumors circulated that Hoxie planned to sell the Brooklyn Campus. Many thought this was Hoxie's cruel retaliation, although from the point of view of a chancellor wanting to build a great university on Long Island, the plan made sense. A sale could bring in the money needed to create the graduate university. Usually college campuses are hard to sell, but the expanding City University of New York wanted a home for Baruch College and here was a ready-made campus.

Students and faculty at Brooklyn could not look at the situation that way. They were incensed.[19] Under the chairmanship of Professor Robert Spector, the faculty organized itself and the students in opposition.[20] For months, they so peppered the news media that New Yorkers became increasingly interested in and sympathetic toward the Brooklyn Campus and its mission of giving under-served students the opportunity to change their lives. The activists persuaded the New York State Joint Legislative Committee on Higher Education to hold public hearings on the proposed sale. Along with supporters from the United Federation of Teachers, the American Association of University Professors and members of Congress, they showed that CUNY could accommodate only 3,000 of the 7,000 students then on the Brooklyn Campus, that programs valuable to the city like nursing would be discontinued, that students with weaker high school grades, often from the poorer schools, would be forever deprived of the chance to catch up on their education. Among those presenting testimony was the Brooklyn Campus Student Organization of Black Unity whose spokesperson, Harold Charles, said: "Black students stand to lose more than ... other students.... Coming for the most part from the ghetto, [they have found the Brooklyn Center] one of the few avenues of higher education open to them in the City."[21]

The Committee's resulting advisory report favored continuation of the Brooklyn Center: it gave thousands of

> "Chanting, sign-carrying students kept Hoxie from reaching his office."

1957
Operation Rebound: the Long Island University Brooklyn basketball team re-enters intercollegiate games after a six-year suspension.

1958
The first atomic submarine, the *Nautilus*, travels under the North Pole.

students a "unique educational opportunity" that they would lose if the sale went through, and rather than being the financial drain Hoxie alleged, it had surplus funds that Hoxie was siphoning off for use at Post and Southampton.[22]

Hoxie argued (correctly as it turned out) that the City University would soon take away Brooklyn's students through its anticipated open admissions policy and its free tuition. While he continued negotiations for the sale, the Center's faculty and students renewed their protests with a march across the Brooklyn Bridge to City Hall. Months later, after the Center had attempted legal suits, appealed to the State Board of Regents, and received an open letter of support from Mayor John Lindsay, the City Board of Higher Education decided not to purchase the Brooklyn Campus after all, and the events of those two years became unforgettable history.

Meanwhile Hoxie and the campus provosts had to contend with Long Island University students' responses to nationwide events. The civil rights movement that began in the 1950s had formulated fundamental ideas that would inform subsequent protest movements. It questioned the status quo represented by segregation and asserted people's rights to self-determination. A host of later movements, each with many sub-groups, would question other status quos and argue for additional forms of self-determination. Among these were movements against the Vietnam War and on behalf of rights for students, women, gays and the disabled.

All three campuses at Long Island University had protests against the Vietnam War, but C.W. Post's were the most contentious. Despite some liberal tendencies indicated by its enthusiastic greeting of Robert Kennedy in 1960 and support for a lecture on Islam by Muhammad Ali in 1968, its administration and students were politically the most conservative and least likely to protest established ways.

Consequently, when a small group of faculty members organized Post's first opposition to the Vietnam War, the main speaker, mathematics professor Ralph Knopf, faced students who blared music throughout the speech and threw eggs at him. It took considerable courage for the faculty and some students to continue daily protests. Ultimately, however, after National Guardsmen killed four students at Kent State University in May 1970, many more students flocked to the protests on Post's Great Lawn. These disturbances caused administrators to close the Campus for nearly a week.

Southampton's and Brooklyn's anti-war actions brought less campus turmoil, perhaps because both campuses were more accustomed to protest. Faculty and students from both had marched in Southern civil rights protests. Southampton's several hundred faculty and students had vigorously opposed the attempted sale of Brooklyn. They continued to create their brand new college with little support from the central administration. Like their contemporaries elsewhere, the "passive majority" disregarded the "Berkeley-type" struggles for civil rights and peace, but they were urged by the liberal editors of the Windmill to debate an array of contemporary issues: the conditions of workers in the local potato fields, the very existence of a very small group connected with the national Students for a Democratic Society, "free universities" created in opposition to the institutionalized institutions, some black American athletes' refusals to stand respectfully for the national anthem, and even abortion and contraception years before abortion was legalized in 1973.

Mayor John Lindsay, a popular supporter of the Brooklyn Campus, shown here during a visit. The telegram reflects his ardent views.

People on the Brooklyn Campus were the most likely to take protests in their stride because of Birenbaum's earlier encouragement and their own urban experience. At times, their actions were well ahead of national trends. In 1966-67, for instance, well before the disability rights movement emerged elsewhere in the country, disabled students Judy Heumann and Marilyn Savilon founded the LIU Handicapped Independence Movement to urge that the Campus be made accessible. Responding to their actions, Acting Provost William "Buck" Lai asked Professor Theodore F. Childs to create the now-renowned Special Education Services program that has since graduated hundreds of students. (Heumann went on to become Assistant Secretary of Special Education and Rehabilitative

---

1959 
The Brentwood Campus is founded in Suffolk County.
R. Gordon Hoxie is named dean of C.W. Post.

1960 
John F. Kennedy becomes the first Roman Catholic U.S. president.

Post students of the Vietnam era added their voices to nationwide protests.

Services in the Clinton administration.)

During the later years of campus protest, students at Long Island University, like students everywhere, also began to question the University's absolute authority over academic matters and its parental role. The students demanded greater freedom of expression, a say in the content of courses, programs and governance, and freedom from parietal rules. The actual changes instituted varied by campus, but all added new courses in subjects ranging from black history to environmentalism, made some degree requirements more flexible, and dropped others, like gym and even foreign languages.

By the early '70s, dress codes and dormitory rules had been transformed. Students could wear what they wanted. Dormitory residents had no curfews and could have guests at any hour in coed dormitories. Post's campus head, President Robert L. Payton, faced parent and community criticism for lax dormitory rules, but in November 1969, he announced that he would not "play dad." *In loco parentis* was dead.

George Sutton, the former head of campus security at C.W. Post and now vice president for legal services and University counsel, described how quickly the University renounced its parental responsibilities. In the early '60s a horrified librarian called security to remove a shocking, unnamed object from a closed carrel. Fearing the worst, Sutton investigated and found a pin-up photograph. "Three years later," he said, "you couldn't shock anybody." Ideas about freedom of expression caused jackets and dresses to be replaced by jeans and sweat shirts, men grew their hair long, women used language that previously men had used in private, the photograph of a streaker graced the cover of the Pioneer and the radio station broadcast a "sound portrait of an orgasm." Some people interpreted such behavior as undisciplined and self-centered; others protested that young people should be able to control their own lives.

The transformation in campus culture was overseen primarily by the presidents (formerly provosts) of the Brooklyn, Post and Southampton campuses. But campus protests were not these men's major worries. They, along with their faculties and staffs, grew to believe that Hoxie was draining the campuses to provide the financial and educational support for the grand university he was planning. Post's faculty members had so little use for his central administration that they demanded the University sell Hoxie's off-campus home and the buildings that served as the Administrative Center. Eventually the trustees, who for the most part had supported Hoxie, became convinced the University could not find the many millions of dollars needed for his plans. In 1968, they asked him to resign.

The University Hoxie left had little sense of direction. The individual campuses had little commitment to the larger institution and more and more were talking about separation. Each campus ran its own undergraduate and, despite the University's graduate deans, its own graduate programs. Only the financial offices at the University Center were consistently drawing the institution together. Centrifugal and centripetal forces had always pulled at the institution. Now centrifugal

1962
John H.G. Pell is appointed chancellor of Long Island University.
President Richard L. Conolly and his wife die in a plane crash.
The Trustees approve creation of Southampton College.
John Glenn becomes the first American to orbit the Earth.
Racial tensions in the U.S. escalate, and President John F. Kennedy sends federal troops to enforce integration at the University of Mississippi after rioting occurs.

1963
Southampton College opens with Dr. Edward C. Glanz as provost.
JFK is assassinated; Martin Luther King gives "I Have a Dream" speech.

forces were winning. During three years, three interim administrations faltered over the question of whether the University should meet these problems as one institution or as separate colleges.

Transitions Under Chancellor Albert Bush-Brown: 1971-1984

In 1971, the trustees appointed Albert Bush-Brown to bring the University together. Chancellor Bush-Brown's Princeton Ph.D. dissertation had been about college and university architecture in the nineteenth century, and he had been a professor and administrator at a number of northeastern U.S. colleges and universities including M.I.T. Like his predecessors he moved easily among the local elite. A man of considerable charm but uncertain ambitions and strategies, he soon became preoccupied by the grave financial restraints that gripped all American institutions of higher education.

Student enrollments declined as an economic recession reduced incomes, inflation increased costs and the proportion of college-age people declined. Increased government demands for record keeping, combined with rapid scientific and technical developments, raised operating costs even further. All across the country private colleges with small endowments were closing. In New York State, they faced still other problems: the State University expanded, offering its state-subsidized college alternative, and in 1969 City University, which charged no tuition, adopted an open admissions policy. During the '70s and '80s, serious declines in enrollment plunged parts of the University into poverty and brought severe restraints to the rest. Everywhere enrollments sagged: Brooklyn's plummeted.

Bush-Brown had expected to help the University's components stimulate and support each other. Now its very survival depended on such unity. As parts of one institution, the components had less overhead because they could share business and financial operations costs. The administration could use surpluses in one or more parts of the network to support the others. For instance, the non-residential programs at Brentwood, Westchester and Rockland fared well financially because they had much less overhead. In the '70s their surpluses, combined with Post's, often made up for deficits at Brooklyn. For the first half of the '80s, the later years of Bush-Brown's administration, only the non-residential campuses had surpluses.

The reallocation policy did indeed benefit the University as a whole, even as individual campuses objected to the University redistributing their funds. However, the University had to do more. To save money, Bush-Brown delayed building construction and cut all other conceivable expenditures right down to heating, lighting and postage.

"Now the University's very survival depended on unity."

At Brooklyn, the University froze faculty salaries, stopped awarding tenure and moved some tenured faculty into administration. Some professors were sent to teach at C.W. Post, whose campus culture and departmental programs were so different that neither hosts nor visitors were comfortable. Very, very few could find jobs elsewhere because other colleges and universities were not hiring, either. The knowledge that Hoxie had almost sold the Campus, and that Bush-Brown still could, contributed to the sense of impending doom. Even the digital clock, which for years had topped the Dime Savings Bank near the Campus, failed to keep time.

Faculty members at the College of Pharmacy had even more to fear. During the mid-'70s, both Columbia and Fordham Universities had closed their schools of pharmacy, in part because of serious enrollment declines. A comparable threat was aggravated at Pharmacy by its students' unwillingness to travel to the Lafayette Avenue building in the heart of a Bedford-Stuyvesant neighborhood that then was in rapid decline.

C.W. Post's faculty felt more secure, but Southampton's worried because their campus had not found its financial footing. Both groups had to accept University cutbacks, although not without objection. At Southampton, students vigorously protested the anticipated dismissal of instructors. The campus

1964

R. Gordon Hoxie is appointed chancellor of Long Island University.

The Beatles' "I Wanna Hold Your Hand" becomes a hit.

1965

The University's Administration Center moves from Brooklyn to Brookville.

Friends World College is founded by Quakers in Lloyd Harbor, NY.

could not afford to hire new faculty members. On both campuses, many untenured faculty members lost their jobs. For those who survived, tenure was replaced by Contractual Continuation of Employment — a guarantee of annual employment so long as the University needed their services. Salary increases for faculty were held down as they were for staff and administrators. Almost no money was available for the activities that nurture intellectual vitality like attending conferences, developing new programs or buying library books. Campuses competed vigorously for small awards from the University's McGrath Fund, established by a board member, to support activities for academic enrichment like a lecture by Twyla Tharp on dance, a conference on Native Americans, and a conference on bioethics and human rights. Gifts from other board members endowed the annual Scholarly Achievement Awards given to outstanding faculty members.

The lean times brought complaints, freely-distributed blame and, one day, even an editorial in the Post Pioneer objecting to the University's celebration of its 50th anniversary in 1976. But the administration continued with its celebration and people on individual campuses remained active and involved, unlike those in the "sad, gray dispirited colleges" one faculty member reported encountering elsewhere.

Each campus leaned on its strengths, enhancing old programs and creating new ones, often using money from federal and local grants. All offered the same basic majors and all had special programs in cooperative education, academic reinforcement and honors. Under Campus President Edward A. Clark, Brooklyn increased its offerings in the expanding health-related professions with new programs for which campus leaders had identified not only student demand but sometimes even donors. These were physical therapy, physicians' assistant training, community health and health care administration, athletic training and sports sciences. After the College of Pharmacy moved in 1976 from Lafayette Avenue to the Brooklyn Campus, these enterprises joined Pharmacy and became part of the Arnold & Marie Schwartz College of Pharmacy and Health Sciences in buildings funded largely by the Schwartzes. From its new location and under the leadership of Dean Arthur G. Zupko, the College could play a more active role in the work of its natural associates like local hospitals, and its students could easily take their required liberal arts classes in courses taught by Brooklyn Campus faculty. The College still had, and has, its own commencement. Faculty members still had their own union. The board became a council of overseers whose members advised the dean and University officers and occupied five seats on the University board of trustees.

Albert Bush-Brown.

Elsewhere on the Brooklyn Campus, the distinguished special education program, with over 300 disabled students, now offered a master's degree for high school teachers. In 1975, special education moved to the Library Learning Center whose construction, like the growth of the program, illustrated how resourceful administrators enabled the Campus to grow. They found federal, state and city money available for the development of depressed urban areas and built the Center with funds from both a federal grant and the Schwartzes. Local government officials recognized that the University's campus was crucial to their plans for the redevelopment of the downtown area. Indeed, in one report they said, "Undoubtedly the vitality of Long Island University is key to the development of downtown Brooklyn." With the officials' help, the Brooklyn Campus received a federal low-interest loan to refurbish its residence hall. The athletics program finally received on-campus basketball space with a court created within the largely unchanged body of the Paramount Theater.

The Business School enhanced its enrollments and helped local banks by giving annual twelve-week courses

1966
Two handicapped students form the LIU Handicapped Independence Movement, resulting in the Special Education Services program that now boasts hundreds of graduates.

The National Organization for Women (NOW) is founded.

1967
The University establishes its first Ph.D. program in Brooklyn: Clinical Psychology.

Strikes by Brooklyn and Southampton students protest Hoxie's dismissal of vice president and provost of the Brooklyn Campus, William M. Birenbaum.

(with tuition paid for by the banks) to fifty or more minority high school seniors who might be interested in banking careers. Throughout the '70s, the Campus ran programs in sociology and in guidance and counseling for military personnel from the U.S. Army Chaplain Center and School at Fort Wadsworth, Staten Island. And, of course, each year it continued to administer the George Polk Awards for journalism.

With financial help from the city, the University constructed University Plaza, an elongated triangle of grass and trees along Flatbush Avenue that replaced two ugly gas stations. Although a few faculty members laughingly sighed over losing such a convenient place to get their cars serviced and, then as now, some students needed to be disabused of the idea that these kinds of improvements were funded with their tuition money rather than independent sources, the Campus was greatly pleased with the changes.

At Post, where Edward J. Cook was president, the Roth Graduate School of Business continued to grow. It opened the School of Professional Accountancy, introduced a master's degree in public administration, established a Tax Institute, began a business ethics program and founded the Center for Economic Research, which soon was answering 1,600 calls a year from Long Island businesses. The criminal justice program, established in 1971, met with an enthusiastic response. Soon it was offering graduate courses in Manhattan to New York City police personnel and its graduate and undergraduate students totaled more than 800. Special sessions like the Weekend College for working adults increased dramatically. As a campus, C.W. Post was eligible for fewer government grants than Brooklyn but more likely to receive gifts from wealthy donors. One enabled the campus radio station to air programs on Shakespeare and government through which listeners could, after writing papers and taking exams, earn college credit for college courses.

Performances at the Hillwood Commons auditorium and elsewhere on campus were making C.W. Post a cultural center for Long Island. One night in 1978, Hillwood's dome suddenly collapsed under 16 inches of snow. People going out to shovel in the morning found the campus skyline completely changed. Bush-Brown, aided by substantial donations, replaced the building with a larger, more modern concert theater that could accommodate large ensembles like the New York Philharmonic Orchestra. Some years later, under President David J. Steinberg, it received its permanent name, Tilles Center for the Performing Arts, after the developer Gilbert Tilles and his wife, Rose, who gave significant support. The Center was soon dubbed by Newsday "the Lincoln Center of Long Island." The adjoining Hillwood Recital Hall provided a more intimate space for chamber music concerts by groups like the Aeolian Players. Thousands of visitors attended the annual American Arts Festival. Others attended The Hutton House Lectures to explore topics like "Medieval Literature" and "Tutankhamen."

At the far end of the Island, Southampton's president Harry A. Marmion and the marine biology program welcomed the donation of a three-acre ecological preserve on the bayfront near the Marine Station. Students from the marine biology program distinguished themselves year after year, winning 35 Fulbright awards for study in foreign countries. The College also developed its SEAmester program, a nine-week session for undergraduates with classes in oceanography, marine science, maritime history, literature of the sea and navigation. The program is conducted aboard a schooner sailing along the eastern coast of the United States and the Caribbean on which the students serve as supplementary crew.

When sociology professor Chuck Hitchcock joined the faculty in 1969 after serving as a Peace Corps volunteer in Bangladesh, he embraced the notion of experiential learning that the SEAmester implied. As part of his course on social stratification in the Hamptons, students took on jobs like volunteering on the Shinnecock reservation or, in one case, as a sous-chef for a wealthy family. The new winter session continued the emphasis: students who could afford to travel

> *"Mostly I appreciated the keen interest professors took in their students."*

1968
CUNY drops its plan to purchase the Brooklyn Campus.
R. Gordon Hoxie resigns as Long Island University chancellor.
Robert F. Kennedy and Martin Luther King are assassinated.

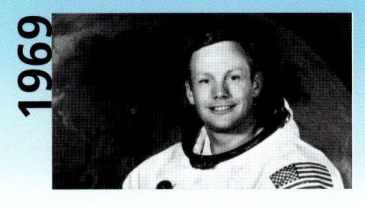

1969
Neil Armstrong becomes the first man to walk on the moon.
The Woodstock music festival in the Catskill Mountains draws record-breaking crowds.

The float moved on but youth and spirit were forever captured in this photo. Here the top ten homecoming king and queen candidates are seen riding by and riding high in a pre-game parade. The year: 1983. The place: C.W. Post

could continue their learning, accompanied by faculty members, in places like Mexico. These courses and programs expanded the experiential learning component of the College that today is central to the whole University's pedagogical strategy.

Work in the fine arts lends itself to the same approach and, drawing upon the artistic and literary scene in the Southampton area, the College instituted a degree in the fine arts. It brought exhibitions to the Campus with accompanying critics, museum curators and dealers, and it introduced the Windmill lecture series for off-campus residents.

These programs defined the special educational style adopted by Southampton's faculty. Phyllis Neuman S'80 referred to the intimacy of the Campus: "Everybody seemed to know everybody else. The guy in the fisherman's sweater who hung out in the Marine Science Center, the girl with the long hair always studying in the Tar. . . . Mostly I appreciated the keen interest that most professors took in their students."

The sense of community could lead to campus-wide jokes. In the early '70s, marine science students kidnapped a gigantic whale jawbone from its locked home in the Natural Science building. In a ransom note, they threatened to apply their own special chemical formula to shrink it. When, after a few days, they had received no reply, they left a small replica of a whale jawbone on the division director's desk with a threat that further application of the formula would reduce the department icon to an ornament on a key chain. When the ransom (perhaps a beer party) was paid, the restored and gift-wrapped jawbone appeared, not in its place, but squeezed into the director's tiny office.

As Southampton, C.W. Post and Brooklyn were developing campus cultures, the University's regional campuses continued developing their offerings for "non-traditional"

1970
Student protests close the C.W. Post Campus for nearly a week.

1971
Albert Bush-Brown becomes Long Island University's chancellor.

"Masterpiece Theater," "All in the Family," and "The Electric Company" premiere on television.

male and female students who wanted to earn promotions, change careers or re-enter the workforce after raising children. All the University's main campuses sponsored evening, weekend and summer programs for students who could not attend in the daytime, and the off-campus sites offered such programs almost exclusively. By the early 1980s the campuses at Brentwood, in Suffolk County, and in Rockland and Westchester Counties were offering mostly graduate programs to local residents in fields like accounting, taxation, health administration, criminal justice and education. Students could complete their Long Island University degrees without adding hours of extra commuting to their workdays. In parts of Long Island where students had greater needs for undergraduate education, the University had dozens of extension programs at which a person could take two years' worth of courses before moving to one of the three main campuses to finish up.

The many women participating in the off-campus programs of the 1970s and 1980s responded to the dramatic social changes achieved by the women's movement that accompanied the later stages of the student and civil rights protests of the 1960s. Women's roles were transformed beyond housewife and mother. More women students, faculty and staff members appeared in student and university publications as participants in business administration programs, awards recipients, women's studies majors and athletes. Now that federal legislation required equal opportunity for women athletes their numbers burgeoned. At C.W. Post, a second floor was added to the Field House.

Unions, Strikes and Faculty Autonomy

In 1972, the administration and the Brooklyn faculty union completed the first collectively bargained faculty agreement at a private university in the United States. It was a long time coming, because at Long Island University, as elsewhere in academe, faculty and staff members generally are more attached to their institutions than employees elsewhere; they can see how their work furthers the university's purpose of helping students learn and develop. Their shared work and vision encourages camaraderie and a sense of belonging. This loyalty and commitment, however, have not prevented academicians from wanting more pay and better working conditions or unions to negotiate those matters. Indeed, unions are one more example of the increased responsibilities that fell on Long Island University's central administration during the '70s and '80s. Some unions, like those for faculty members, were limited to a particular campus. Others, like unions for clerical workers, maintenance workers and skilled tradesmen, tended to be university wide.

Unions may have taken root with particular speed at Long Island University because of the legacy of distrust engendered by the disputes during Hoxie's years. But the growth in the 1970s also was part of rapid unionization by faculty unions in both public and private institutions. The small wage increases of a weak economy partly spurred the movement. Perhaps more significantly, faculty members objected to the old styles of personal but autocratic administration then found in many institutions. Presidents, deans and chairman determined a person's salary, rank, tenure status and workload, and an unfairly treated faculty member had little recourse.

Long Island University had been no exception. Professor Andreas Zavitsas of Brooklyn observed that "in the late sixties chairs were autocrats. The deans said how much was available; they gave the raises. In a lot of departments, they rewarded people they liked. For example, the psychologists with the 'right' interests got big raises." Significant intercampus differences in salaries, rank, tenure and workloads exacerbated feuds between the administration and the campuses. During those years of large deficits, the University could ill afford to spend money on anything: it could not respond to all these needs. Complaints multiplied with time. When Bush-Brown became president in 1971, only buildings and grounds employees were unionized; by the time he left office in 1984, eight unions had been added, representing clerical employees, faculty members and administrators.

"Post's union president called what became a 20-day strike. The semester started three weeks late."

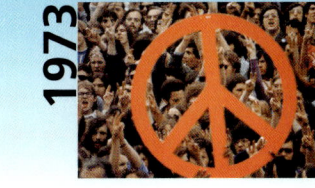

1972

The administration and a Brooklyn faculty union complete the first collectively bargained faculty agreement at a U.S. private university.

1973

Direct American involvement in Vietnam ends.

1974
Richard Nixon becomes the first U.S. president to resign office.

1975
The Westchester Campus for graduate studies opens.
The last American troops leave Vietnam.

The unions negotiated with Bush-Brown's right hand man, Executive Vice President David Newton. The contracts that resulted in the 1970s addressed very different campus situations. The Brooklyn faculty, struggling to keep their campus going, negotiated fiercely over proposed faculty layoffs, reallocations of faculty from overstaffed departments to the Post Campus and into administrative positions, and a proposed moratorium on salaries. Low pay, especially in the context of salary inequities with Post, precipitated such a long strike in 1979 that the University almost had to cancel classes for the semester and suffer the subsequent financial losses. The Brooklyn faculty entered the '80s with substantially lower salaries than their colleagues in the rest of the University.

Post's situation was different. With high enrollments that through the 1970s included the Brentwood students, it was the only segment of the University not running a deficit. A successful but bloody battle over tenure for junior members propelled the Post faculty to form its union in 1973. Despite a brief strike, that union in 1975 had to accept Contractual Continuation of Employment. In addition to matters of job security, Post professors had other sources of discontent. They objected to the financial restrictions inhibiting the development of innovative programs and to administrative constraints on academic decision-making.

Post's union president, John Turner, called what became a 20-day strike in September, 1977, which in turn caused the University to restructure classes for the term to make sure students received the appropriate state-mandated hours of instruction when the semester started three weeks late. Eventually, the faculty received modest guarantees of job security and pay increases. This and later contracts eventually removed most on-campus inequities in faculty salaries and established a step scale by rank and years of service — yet left a disparity in salaries that the Brooklyn Campus was still working to resolve in 2001. (The question of faculty authority to share in academic decision-making has been addressed through the years in both union contracts and periodic revisions of the University Statutes.)

The bitterness of the 1977 C.W. Post strike and the tensions between University and College left a bad taste in everyone's mouth and, for the Post faculty, highlighted again the question of whether one university could meet the needs of such diverse communities. For its part, Southampton's faculty has been negotiating contracts since 1974, but compared with union leaders at Post and Brooklyn, its negotiators have had little leverage. The College is small and has almost always operated at a financial loss. The provisions of its contracts have tended to echo Post's.

The differing employment pictures mirrored the way Bush-Brown's administration ended, with each of the University's member campuses still accustomed to dealing with its own problems rather than working together as a single institution. Each also had a distinct identity derived from its history, geography, students and resources — Brooklyn urban, Post suburban, Southampton exurban.

Yet whatever campus they attended, students again and again referred to Long Island University as a place that gave them "opportunity" — the chance to attend college despite difficult circumstances, to start college in their twenties or thirties, to complete an unfinished bachelor's degree or to earn a professional master's or doctorate.

Managing Complexities: President David J. Steinberg

When David J. Steinberg arrived at Long Island University in 1985, he brought years of experience as a Harvard-trained professor who had earned an international scholarly reputation in Philippines history and as an outstanding administrator and fundraiser at Brandeis University. He came understanding university life, knowing how to administer an academic institution and raise funds to sustain it. In addition — a qualification peculiarly suited to a president who has to travel constantly between campuses — he moves and thinks very quickly. His personal history echoed many students' own. His paternal grandfather migrated from the European shtetl to Ocean Avenue in Brooklyn. His father,

President David J. Steinberg

1976 The College of Pharmacy moves from Lafayette Avenue to the Brooklyn Campus.
Stephen Wozniek and Steven Jobs found Apple Computer.

1977 The SEAmester program begins at Southampton College.

1978 The John Steinbeck Room (a writers' resource center) opens at the Southampton College Library.

New leadership for the University arrived in 1985 with the appointment of President David J. Steinberg, a Harvard-educated historian and noted Southeast Asia scholar. He is shown on inauguration day proudly parading in downtown Brooklyn flanked by University Chairman William Zeckendorf, Jr. (left) and Harvard's president, Derek Bok.

1979 Nuclear-related accident occurs at Three Mile Island in Pennsylvania.

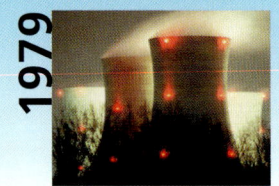

Oil shortages create long lines at gas stations. Paul Volcker, new chairman of the Federal Reserve, moves to stop inflation by raising interest rates.

1980 WPBX LONG ISLAND'S PUBLIC RADIO STATION 88.3FM

WPBX-FM, Southampton College radio station, goes on the air.

The Rockland Campus for graduate studies opens.

Milton Steinberg, became the distinguished rabbi of New York City's Park Avenue Synagogue. Though Steinberg's academic career at first took him out of New York City, it finally returned him to Brooklyn. There, in the fall of 1985, he held his inauguration at the Brooklyn Academy of Music and led 700 Long Island University students, faculty and staff members in an inspiriting parade up Flatbush Avenue Extension to the Brooklyn Campus.

By having an inaugural that gathered the whole University in Brooklyn, Steinberg made clear his determination to clarify the University's identity as an institution serving the ordinary people of the Long Island and New York City region. Less apparent at the ceremonies was a second determination: to restore the University's financial health.

Steinberg rejected the idea heard so often in the University's past that it would benefit from the sale of one or both of the financially-strapped Brooklyn and Southampton Campuses. College campuses usually cost a considerable amount of money to close down because few people want to buy them and the seller has to pay off major financial obligations like long term debt and tenure contracts. (Hoxie's planned sale of Brooklyn would have been the exception because the expanding City University of New York would have paid a good price for a ready-made campus.) Moreover, the Board of Regents of New York State can prohibit a sale on the grounds that the local community needs the institution. Instead of selling any piece of the University, Steinberg focused on revitalizing the whole.

Any such effort had to take account of three decades of profound change in American higher education. The country's colleges and universities had completed their transformation from the simple, informal places of the past to the complex administrative units of the 21st century. Indeed, the list of responsibilities continues to grow. Nowadays a university must evaluate and incorporate ever-changing technologies; guide students through the constantly changing mass of loan and scholarship programs emerging from federal, state and other sources; respond to government demands for audits and reviews of student education and financial matters; negotiate with several kinds of unions; and prepare its departments, programs, schools and the whole institution for accreditation reviews by state, regional and professional groups. (At Long Island University, for example, a final report to the Middle States accrediting organization weighs over 30 pounds.) Throughout the country's colleges and universities all these responsibilities now accompany the essential work of teaching.

These changes brought greatly increased costs at a time when flagging enrollments once again reduced income. At

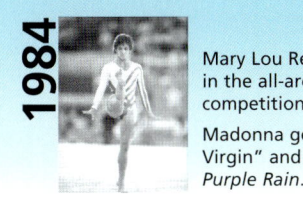

> "The great threat to higher education and society is that more and more young people will find the cost of college beyond their means."

1981 The C.W. Post Concert Theater (later, Rose and Gilbert Tilles Center for the Performing Arts) opens, replacing the Dome Auditorium which had collapsed.

1982 AT&T is divided into several companies.

1984 Mary Lou Retton wins the gold medal in the all-around women's gymnastics competition at the Los Angeles Olympics. Madonna gets her first hit with "Like a Virgin" and Prince releases his album *Purple Rain*.

Long Island University it seemed that only the stringent economic measures adopted during the Bush-Brown years were saving it from disaster. Indeed, by the mid-1980s the University's cumulative deficit was inching downward from its mid-1970s high. Many felt that if all belts stayed tightened the institution would break free from debt. However, Steinberg and others argued that the campuses were growing less and less attractive as places to learn. Everywhere, established academic programs needed to be overhauled and new programs introduced. Years of neglect had to be made up for in the libraries, laboratories and technological facilities. The physical plant badly needed renovation, and, most expensive of all, the campuses needed new buildings.

Instead of continuing to reduce the debt, Steinberg convinced the board to undertake deficit spending, as he later put it, to "restart the engine and buy time." Mary M. Lai, the vice president for finance, a devout Catholic, went home and prayed. She recalled that "prayer helped, but I did more than pray." After more conventional lending sources had turned the University down, she obtained insurance and a commitment from underwriters to sell $17 million in taxable bonds which would later be converted to tax-exempt bonds through New York State's Dormitory Authority when the University's finances improved. The five-year deficit spending plan worked. Increased enrollments and reduced attrition enabled the university to balance its budget and, in 1996, to eliminate its cumulative deficit. Those achievements, together with successful fund raising, so improved the University's credit rating that it could borrow for further plant improvements at a much more favorable interest rate than had been possible five years earlier.

The University's financial problems had other roots. During the same decades that brought higher costs and decreased enrollments to American universities there was increased questioning of the liberal intellectual view that, in 1926, stimulated the University's founders to work for and contribute to the institution. This was the view that higher education is a public good to be supported by the public, that colleges and universities support democracy and contribute to social growth by training professionals and advancing knowledge, a view that says society gains as much from the university as the people who earn degrees.

The public universities have reaped the most financial advantages from this conviction and its result, government support of higher education, but Long Island University also has received support. In the 1940s, the GI Bill of Rights gave significant funding to many of its students. Later graduates benefited from the higher education legislation of Lyndon B. Johnson's presidency and Nelson A. Rockefeller's governorship of New York State. In the 1980s and 1990s, however, assistance to students diminished greatly following reductions in programs like the federal Pell and Higher Education Opportunity Grants and the New York State Tuition Assistance Program, Higher Education Resource Services and "Bundy" Aid. Similarly, government support for everything from new programs to new buildings has diminished.

Today the great threat to higher education and to society itself is that more and more young people will find the cost of college beyond their means, and that the vast majority of colleges will have inadequate funds to support them (as well as to keep their institutions up to date). Long Island University will be among the universities particularly affected because most of its students come from families with moderate incomes,[23] making them highly dependent on loans and scholarships. At each of the University's three residential campuses, over 80 percent of the undergraduate students receive financial aid. As the idea of education as a social good fades, student aid has come more frequently in the form of loans rather than outright grants,[24] so that the very students the University chose to serve in 1926 risk being excluded. Here the economic significance of race becomes distressingly apparent. Because black, Hispanic and many immigrant Asian families in the New York region earn less than whites, their children are the more likely to be deprived of a college education. For

"The University revitalized its campuses."

1985 David Steinberg inaugurated as president of Long Island University.

1986 Gilbert and Rose Tilles' gift to the University of $1.2 million for the concert hall sets a new record for giving to a Long Island arts organization.

1988 The trustees approve the Long Island University Plan.

the present at least, on each of Long Island University's residential campuses, student body breakdowns by race and ethnicity repeat remarkably closely the proportions in the counties where they are located.

Although private universities are more seriously affected by changes in government programs because their tuition, operating and building costs are not subsidized by the state, even the public institutions are seriously underfunded.

Historically, presidents of public institutions have sought money from state governments; presidents of private universities have sought out individual donors. These days they work in the same arenas. In particular, public universities compete with private for the largess of individual donors.

President Steinberg is no exception to the rule that every university today treats fundraising as a major responsibility. By the time the University's seventy-fifth anniversary year began in December of 2001, he was expecting its endowment to be over $50 million. Compared with the billion dollar endowments of large research universities this figure is small, but it is a far larger buffer against hard times than the $4.4 million available when he arrived and compares well to the nest eggs of the other universities on Long Island. During these same years, Steinberg raised an additional $100 million for academic programs and for construction and renovation of buildings, and the University spent $200 million on its physical plant.

When a university president is joined by active trustees, more funds are raised. The Long Island University board under Steinberg has indeed become involved. Almost all of these men and women, numbering 41 in 2000, live on Long Island and work there or in New York City. Over a third are alumni. Since they know the University's needs and the region's resources, they not only make personal gifts but also contact other people who want to help. Four trustees serve as campus Chancellors — one for each residential campus and Brentwood, Westchester and Rockland together. They and other board members are often seen around the University attending activities ranging from Pharmacy's Retail Drug Institute dinner to a soiree on the Great Lawn of the C.W. Post Campus to a day-long Founders' Day celebration ending with a clambake at Southampton.

Using major gifts from donors and government-backed borrowing, at the turn of the 21st century the University revitalized its campuses. Brooklyn received the Zeckendorf building for the health sciences, linked to the rest of the campus by a bridge and by a theme of circular motifs that repeat exterior decorations on the old Paramount theater building. Appropriately, three floors of this building belong to Pharmacy, whose dean, Stephen M. Gross, has raised substantial funds for health-related buildings on campus through his ties to the pharmaceutical industry. The Campus's School of Education and student services moved into the Jeanette and Edmund T. Pratt Jr. Center for Academic Studies, which puzzled old timers by materializing in a seemingly non-existent space. (The area once held a generating station for the BMT subway line.) At C.W. Post, after a wearying reprise of the community opposition in the original "Battle of Brookville," construction of a recreation center and pool, also partially financed by a Pratt gift, got underway in the fall of 2000. Renovation of Marjorie Merriweather Post's mansion, symbol of the Campus, was scheduled to begin in 2001 thanks to one of several gifts from Gary Winnick P'69 and his wife, Karen. Southampton College completed a new academic center in 1999, its first new building in years, and is preparing for a library expansion thanks to gifts from its Chancellor, Robert Sillerman, and his wife, Laura Baudo Sillerman, through their Tomorrow Foundation.

Brooklyn's new Jeanette and Edmund T. Pratt Jr. Center for Academic Studies, result of a historic gift.

1989 The Berlin Wall begins to be dismantled.

1991 Persian Gulf War begins as the United States and its allies begin bombing Iraq.
Friend's World College joins the University as Friends World Program at Southampton College.
The Dow Jones tops 3000 for the first time, hitting 3004.46 on April 17.

None of these new buildings could be used effectively unless the University grappled with coordinating its seven major and many minor pieces. Since his arrival, Steinberg has worked strenuously to bring them together. The campuses had different academic programs, organizational structures, styles, histories, core curriculums, work loads and requirements for majors and graduation. Further, throughout the University, faculty members, administrators and alumni will always have their individual institutional memories. Shadowing the present are events like the attempt to sell Brooklyn, Brookville's opposition to the creation of C.W. Post College, Southampton's small size and intimacy and Pharmacy's years of real and semi independence. These histories, as much as the differences in students' ethnicity and race and the campuses' distinctive geographical settings, are the roots of the separate identities of Long Island University's individual segments. The president must maintain a delicate balance between maintaining each campus' distinct identity and the monetary and human synergies of coordination.

Such administrative quandaries contributed to faculty-administration unrest in the first part of Steinberg's administration, unrest made very evident in a strike by the C.W. Post faculty and a University Faculty Senate vote of "no confidence" in the president in September, 1985. Since then, the conflicts have been resolved or reduced, among other things by the abolition of University-wide deanships inherited from the later years of Bush-Brown's administration.

Inevitably, a college president must take stands that offend some part of his constituency. In 1995, a passerby at the C.W. Post Campus complained that a Donald Lipski sculpture, in the form of a giant ball of red, white and blue fabric that looked like a flag, desecrated the flag. The resulting brouhaha was small — but it did involve U.S. Congressman Peter T. King, to whom Steinberg wrote:

"Art is indeed in the eye of the beholder, and I recognize your constitutional right to dismiss Mr. Lipski's work. But if you accept that this is an artist attempting in a serious way to make a serious statement, then at least we have found common ground. And, perhaps, you can now understand why a university would welcome public art on its campus."[25]

One much more far-reaching action by the president met far less opposition. In 1991 Long Island University added an important new piece — the Friends World Program. While not focused specifically on the needs of the Long Island and New York region, it is based at Southampton College and stresses the experiential education around which the College and the University revolve. Furthermore, with increasing global integration, its international focus befits the larger program of a modern university.

Friends World was a radical experiment in higher education initiated by Morris Mitchell, a progressive philosopher and follower of John Dewey. He founded Friends World College in 1965 and affiliated it with the Society of Friends — the Quakers. Ten years later it broke with the Quakers and operated as an independent institution until it joined the University with the slightly changed name of Friends World Program. Lewis Greenstein became its director in 1997, and in 1999-2000 for the first time in its history, the program finished the fiscal year in the black.

The self-motivated and socially responsible students attracted to the Friends World Program pursue their educations at Southampton College and at seven overseas sites in China, Costa Rica, England, India, Israel, Japan and Ghana, where they spend a minimum of two years. In the place of traditional courses and grades, students study languages intensively, participate in group projects, keep a portfolio of their learning and receive responses from professors in the form of narrative evaluations. All students choose an area of concentration and submit a project based upon each year's work. Projects have included studies of "Nutrition and Public Health" in Costa Rica, "Conflict Resolution" in Northern Ireland, "Traditional Diagnosis and Treatment" in China, and "Arid-Zone Agriculture" in Israel.

Friends World also offers a popular one-year study abroad

> "You have the most remarkable assortment of imaginative and innovative services for students we have seen in a very long time."

1992 — Southampton College's first annual All for the Sea concert provides marine science scholarships.

1993 — The Hubble Space telescope is repaired.

1994 — *Forest Gump*, starring Tom Hanks, is released.

program in Comparative Religion and Culture, open to students from any accredited college. Students study Confucianism, Taoism and Buddhism in China, Hinduism, Jainism, Sikhism, Buddhism and Islam in India, and Judaism, Islam and Christianity in Israel. Students in this program complete a year-long group project on topics like "Pilgrimage as an Expression of Devotion" and "Buddhist Influence on Japanese Environmental Policy."

Distinctive Education

Every two weeks cars with license plates LIU 1, LIU 2 and so on can be found parked at one of the three residential campuses. These are the days when Steinberg meets with the campus Provosts, the Vice Presidents for Academic Affairs, Finance and University Relations, and the University Counsel. In the early 1990s, their deliberations often focused on reformulating the undergraduate program to meet the needs of the University's student population. These are students with good but not outstanding academic records (except for students in the honors programs on all three residential campuses), who live in the vicinity, who often are the first in their families to attend college, whose families have moderate incomes, who depend on loans and scholarships, and who want a career-oriented education. In all these respects the University's students resemble those at the majority of the United States' 1,200-odd accredited institutions offering four or more years of higher education to a student body of over 1,000 students.

Steinberg and various task forces devised the "LIU Plan" to meet these students' needs. Each campus that enrolls undergraduates — namely the residential campuses — uses a wide range of strategies to enable students to make the most of their college experience. Not all of them were new to the institution. Each campus, especially Southampton, already emphasized one or more of the strategies. As soon as students apply, specially-appointed personnel help them to evaluate their interests, goals and preparation and to choose a program of study. For first-year students University-wide variations of a one-credit orientation course play a critical role. Other staff members help students find funding for their educations.

A second element of the LIU Plan emphasizes the practical and personal importance of having a disciplined as well as a knowledge-filled mind. Students take liberal arts courses outside their professional programs to sharpen their analytic and writing skills as well as to increase their knowledge of the society and the world in which they will work. They also learn the technical languages of our information-based society. The LIU Plan's third element lets students try out and foster their future careers by giving them work experience in their chosen professions. Sometimes this work brings payment for services, thereby helping to fulfill the fourth goal of the Plan, that of making college affordable. Affordability also is achieved through other kinds of co-operative education, through financial aid support and, just as in the 1930s, through course schedules that accommodate working students.

Long Island University students have the opportunity to gain hands-on experience at major corporations. Shown above: a C.W. Post student at Olympus America, Inc.

These and many more improvements contributed to the accolades for student services that the Middle States accreditation agency bestowed in 1993. "We tell you in all honesty: you have the most remarkable assortment of imaginative and innovative services for students we have seen in a very long time. That they should all be found within one institution speaks volumes of the talent and the resourcefulness of your faculty and staff. Their commitment to the well being of students cannot be exaggerated."[26]

Many other aspects of the undergraduate and graduate experience are discussed at the University officers' biweekly meetings. The University constantly revises its specialized programs. In the years around the turn of the 21st century it added 72 programs and discontinued an almost equal number. New programs included a Psy.D. in clinical psychology, complementing a long-established Ph.D. program at Brooklyn,

1995 The first University Professor is appointed: essayist Roger Rosenblatt.

1996 The University eliminates a 35-year cumulative deficit.

1997 Harriet Rothkopf Heilbrunn B'32 and Robert Heilbrunn give the University's first $1 million gift to endow scholarships.

and a Ph.D. in information studies at C.W. Post. The College of Pharmacy and Health Sciences now awards a Ph.D. in pharmaceutics. Both Brooklyn and Post have bachelors' programs in social work and dance.

The University provosts have worked with their campus faculties and their fellow officers on programs that cut across the formal undergraduate and graduate degree offerings. The education schools at Brooklyn and Post have linked centers for schools and students "at risk" in urban neighborhoods or "urbanized" suburbs. The University's National Institute for Hispanic Leadership has developed demonstration programs throughout the institution. As a result, C.W. Post has an accelerated multicultural graduate program in educational administration for Hispanic teachers; Brooklyn has an undergraduate program for 20 Hispanic freshmen involving counseling, internships and mentoring; Southampton has a summer networking program for Hispanic educators; and Brentwood has an outreach project for Hispanics from the local community. Both the Brooklyn and the C.W. Post campuses provide intensive programs in learning the English language. The one in Brooklyn served, among others, hundreds of new immigrants from the former Soviet Union, and has enabled many of them to study pharmacy and other health-related fields. C.W. Post's English-language instruction attracts visiting Korean students who spend two years at Post and two at a Korean university to earn a joint degree.

Two unfunded, marginally related programs illustrate how the institution's supportive culture extends to very small projects that almost seem to emerge spontaneously. Faculty members at both Post and Brooklyn independently hit on the idea of pairing students whose English is weak with native-speaker "conversation partners." Immigrant and foreign students whose shaky language skills may result in poor academic performance learn English, while both partners learn about another culture and have fun.

Another innovation that has pulled the campuses together has been University-wide professorships; so far, one is based at C.W. Post and three at Southampton. These have attracted eminent teachers like the essayist and public television NewsHour commentator Roger Rosenblatt and the jazz pianist Billy Taylor. Each teaches mostly at one campus but gives workshops and lectures at others.

The provosts have made sure each campus is actively involved in the local communities that its students most likely will serve after graduation. Under Provost Gale Stevens Haynes, Brooklyn is collaborating with the Brooklyn Hospital and Medical Center a block away, hoping to use federal and New York State funds from Congress to create a Wellness and Recreation Center for the community. The Campus works directly and indirectly with the same local cultural institutions that in 1926 supported its creation to provide dance programs, theater, film festivals, walking tours, and recent conferences on "Brooklyn as a City Apart" and Jackie Robinson. It has played host to mayoral and senatorial candidates as well as former president Bill Clinton. It has trained hospital and food service employees in the computer skills that can be an immediate help to them and their employees, and encourages them to attend college. During the summer, its annual sculpture exhibitions provoke lively conversations in the main campus courtyard; the shows have included a collection of cast concrete tableware and groves of bronze trees.

> "An accrediting report said the University can be 'justifiably proud of its growth into one of the largest and most comprehensive private universities in the U.S.'"

At C.W. Post, under Provost Joseph Shenker members of the Commuter Student Association have coordinated recreational activities at a center for adults with multiple disabilities. The Campus combines an on-campus day care center with study of early childhood development. Its Hillwood Art Museum reaches out to help local school children study non-western art and culture. The Hutton House lecture program is well into its third decade of offering life-enriching liberal arts courses to hundreds of local residents. Tilles Center is the presenting venue for several of Long Island's leading arts organizations. Financially self-

1998 — Jeanette and Edmund T. Pratt Jr. give $12 million to Long Island University, the largest gift-to-date in the University's history.
The online population numbers between 30-60 million users.

1999 — With a $2.5 million gift from Laura Baudo and Bob Sillerman's Tomorrow Foundation, Southampton's new academic center, Chancellors Hall, opens.

Studying Brooklyn style.

part of their one-credit college introduction course. Later in their careers, the Institute for Regional Research trains students in community understanding by developing and analyzing polling data on issues concerning the five towns of the East End of Long Island. The College works with a Bronx high school that encourages its students to widen their horizons by attending college far outside the city. Students in the Early Childhood Neuroscience track of the popular psychobiology major frequently work with learning disabled students in the Southampton, Hauppauge and Riverhead school districts.

Finally, the University officers closely monitor Long Island University's off-campus offerings. The University's perception of what constitutes the New York City region has expanded up the Hudson to include the Rockland Graduate Campus at Orangeburg and the Westchester Graduate Campus, which now is based in newly-built facilities at Purchase College of the State University. (Brentwood, the oldest of the regional campuses, remains on Long Island.) The University also offers specialized graduate, undergraduate and non-credit-bearing courses at other locations ranging from West Point, further up the Hudson, to Selden on Long Island, to East New York in Brooklyn, to Washington Square in Manhattan and in corporations like Verizon and Symbol Technology.

• • •

In the 75 years since 1926, Long Island University has grown from a small institution to an all-encompassing one. Although everything about the University and the world around it is far more complicated, it has seen no reason to abandon its founders' objectives. It still serves students from Long Island and greater New York. It still welcomes every kind of student. Now, as then, it gives students the liberal arts-based career training they seek. Like its first students, most of its graduates continue to live in the area and contribute their professional skills to the communities the University has always served. As a report in the early 1990s from the Middle States accrediting association put it, the University can be "justifiably proud of its growth into one of the largest and most comprehensive private universities in the U. S."[27] Its convictions and its struggles have borne rich fruit.

supporting, it has the backing of many local people as well as the next generation of the Tilles family. Its programs enrich campus life as students are drawn to watch the Alvin Ailey dancers, a lecture by Barbara Walters or performances by the New York Philharmonic.

Community involvement is equally important at Southampton College. Provost Timothy H. Bishop has watched over the many students who have received National Youth Service Awards for participating in community service projects like working at a shelter for homeless children — as

2000
Large donations multiply: Gifts from Karen and Gary Winnick P'69 reach $11 million.

An international consortium of genetic researchers — collectively called the Human Genome Project — announce a scientific breakthrough: they have completely mapped the genetic code of a human chromosome, raising a plethora of medical, legal and ethical questions.

2001
December 6
Long Island University Anniversary Dinner.

"Many times [the students] challenged me on class procedures, on my facts and interpretations. I loved it, I must say, and this is not sentimental recollection, this is reality. And they loved it, too. They had intense loyalties ... deep dislike of some of us and all-but-adoration for a few of us."

— Professor Leo Gershoy,
History Department, Brooklyn Campus

CHAPTER FOUR
PERSONALITIES

At a black tie University event, board members John P. McGrath (left) and William Zeckendorf Sr. (center) share a moment of levity with President R. Gordon Hoxie (right).

Even governors and university presidents cannot always be sure of a table at popular University events. Here, New York State Governor Averill Harriman (left) and University President Richard L. Conolly (right) carried on unfazed.

Long Island University and its officers reached out to the community by supporting an annual fundraising drive to send needy city children to summer camp. Shown with Tristram Walker Metcalfe (center right), then president of the University, are representatives of several of the churches and groups working with the University.

Eleanor Roosevelt, one of the world's most esteemed women and humanitarians, lectured at the Brooklyn College of Pharmacy. Following her talk, Dean Arthur Zupko showed Mrs. Roosevelt an apothecary jar from the College's collection.

Long Island University "inherited" gardener Sylvester Cangero when it acquired Marjorie Merriweather Post's estate as its new Brookville campus. Cangero was kept on to maintain the magnificent Hillwood property. Shown in a 1966 photo, he was appointed C.W. Post's head gardener and remained so until his 1969 retirement. He tipped his hat to everyone he met.

The Tilles family is noted for its philanthropic commitments on Long Island. Here Roger Tilles, Chair of the University's trustees since 1998, is shown at right with Elliott Sroka (center), the executive director of the University's Tilles Center for the Performing Arts, and Peter Tilles (left), the founding chairman of "Swing for Kids," Tilles Center's annual golf and tennis tournament, which raises funds to support arts programs for thousands of local school children.

A pioneer in establishing civil rights for disabled people, Judith Heumann B'69, H'94, overcame tremendous odds as a physically challenged person. She sued the City of New York after having been denied employment as a teacher because she could not walk. Heumann went on to serve prominently in the Clinton administration as Assistant Secretary for the United States Department of Education's Office of Special Education and Rehabilitation Services.

John P. McGrath, chairman of Long Island University's board of trustees from 1967 to 1974, makes a last-minute adjustment to his cap at a 1978 commencement ceremony.

Before becoming president of Long Island University in 1953, Richard L. Conolly (right) established a distinguished career in the U.S. Navy during two world wars and as president of the Naval War College. Admiral Conolly is shown aboard his ship, the U.S.S. Biscayne, in September of 1943 with a British counterpart, General J. L. Hawksworth.

The mogul's haircut, the admiral's accreditation

The chairman of the Long Island University board was William Zeckendorf Sr., a large bear of a man, famous, handsome, affable, exuding energy and an aura of wealth and power. He was head of the real estate firm of Webb and Knapp and was famous for having put together the land for the United Nations in Manhattan and for ambitious commercial and residential developments in the U.S. and Canada. In the mid 1950s, he was one of the best known power figures in New York.

The Webb and Knapp offices were on Madison Avenue between 45th and 46th Streets. Zeckendorf had a circular office with a terrace. Many LIU board meetings and events were held in those offices. One board meeting was held while the chairman was having a haircut and manicure in the center of the room. He was covered in a white sheet with his hands stretched out before him on the manicure table. The room was rather dark, but he was brightly lighted by down lights on the ceiling. The rest of us were seated around the perimeter of the room in a series of alcoves, each illuminated by a down light. It was like a scene in an opera of a gathering of knights or priests around their leader. Zeckendorf conducted the business of the meeting without batting an eye.

Admiral Conolly was short, slightly rotund, sharp-eyed, thoughtful and very quick. He was accustomed to taking charge in tough situations, making difficult decisions and seeing them through. I learned from the admiral never to be overwhelmed by intimidating circumstances, to keep a cool head, and, having decided on the best possible way out, to pursue it unrelentingly.

When Richard Conolly arrived, the University was not accredited, so he put the institution through the accreditation process. The accreditation team from other institutions had doubts about deficiencies in library holdings and financial resources, but the admiral swore he would remedy them. In the end, the team reportedly said that in granting accreditation they were accrediting him.

— James M. Hester, former president, Long Island University Brooklyn Center, former president, New York University, current president, The Harry Frank Guggenheim Foundation

Memories

Activist and singer Harry Belafonte is shown at a 1991 graduation ceremony in which he was recognized with an honorary degree for his many contributions.

In 1963, Interim Chancellor John H.G. Pell journeyed to Korea to launch the first of the University's alliances with institutions of higher learning in the Far East. He is shown being greeted by his Korean hosts at Chung-ang University.

Lionel L. Richardson B'31, a member of Long Island University's first graduating class, went on to rank first in his medical school class and then into private practice before fulfilling his lifelong sense of mission with a career in public health. Dr. Richardson eventually served with distinction as commissioner of health for Chautauqua County in rural western New York.

John Kanas S'68 (left), the chairman, president and CEO of North Fork Bank, returned to be honored by the University at Tilles Center's 1995 gala. He is shown with Eugene Luntey H'98, chairman of the University's Board of Trustees from 1993 to 1998.

Long Island University trustee Terry Semel B'64 (left), who was recently named chairman, CEO and director of the Internet giant Yahoo!, mingles with President Steinberg (center) and actor Ed Lauter P'60.

Roger Tilles, chair of the University's trustees since 1998, is one of the region's most active civic leaders. He is shown at a campus event with Mary Lai, the university's vice president for finance and treasurer.

In 1998, Jeanette and Edmund T. Pratt Jr. made the largest single gift ever received in the University's history. Mr. Pratt is former chairman and CEO of Pfizer Inc. The Pratts' generosity made it possible to build C.W. Post's recreation center and Brooklyn's new academic and educational building, and to renovate Southampton Hall, the main administration building of the College.

Robert F. X. Sillerman, the executive chairman of The Sillerman Companies, has served as Southampton's chancellor since 1993. He and his wife, Laura Baudo Sillerman, through their Tomorrow Foundation, have provided the lead gifts for Chancellors Hall and the College's new library, and are supporting an exciting writers' conference for summer 2002. Above: The Sillermans in the V.I.P. tent at All for the Sea, the annual benefit concert they created to raise money for marine and environmental science scholarships (see p. 122).

Gary Winnick P'69, one of C.W. Post's most successful alumni, is Chairman and CEO of Pacific Capital Group. He and his wife, Karen, who are devoted to "giving back" to the community, have generously funded the renovation of the Gary Winnick House and the Arnold S. Winnick Student Center at C.W. Post through their Winnick Family Foundation.

Harriet B'32 and Robert Heilbrunn have endowed the Harriet Rothkopf Heilbrunn Endowed Scholarship Fund and the Heilbrunn Urban Teaching Scholars, exemplifying the University's longtime tradition of helping students with financial need to move up in the world.

Southampton's first chancellor, Angier Biddle Duke, served at $1 per year from 1986 to 1991. Chief of protocol for the Kennedy and Johnson administrations, Duke also served as ambassador to Denmark, El Salvador, Spain and Morocco.

The quarter-century chairmanship of William Zeckendorf, Sr. saw Long Island University grow from 800 to 18,000 students. His visionary leadership brought the University to Brookville and Southampton.

Louis Lemberger B'60, H'94 led the Eli Lily team that developed the revolutionary anti-depression drug Prozac.

The Brooklyn College of Pharmacy became a tradition for members of the de Neergaard family. Proudly posing at the family pharmacy in Brooklyn are, at left, William de Neergaard, who served as a trustee of Brooklyn College of Pharmacy, and his son, William F. de Neergaard Ph'47, H'98, who continued the family's service on the University's board beginning in 1979.

The world's most renowned classical and pop artists have appeared on the C.W. Post Campus, at Tilles Center for the Performing Arts. Violinist Itzhak Perlman was the featured performer as the Center marked its 20th year.

"The spirit of Long Island University is alive and thriving"

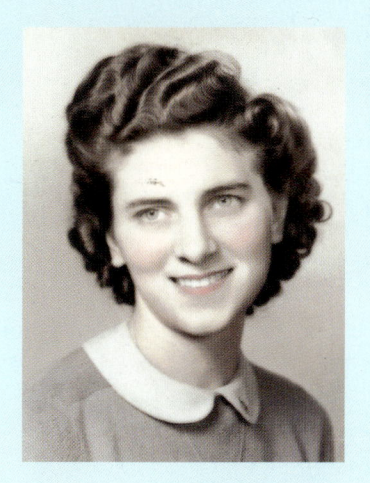

When Long Island University President Tristram Walker Metcalfe called and said he needed her help in handling the University's business affairs, Mary Maneri Lai B'42 knew it was payback time. She was 24 years old, already had a good job in public accounting with Arthur Young & Co. and hated to leave it. But LIU had given her a full scholarship, and if the University needed her, she couldn't say no. She was given the job of bursar.

"I agreed to bring the accounting and business affairs up-to-date and to work for the University for one year," she recalls. That was in 1946. She never left.

Today, she serves Long Island University as vice president of finance and treasurer. In the world of academe she has risen to the heights of her profession. An authentic pioneer in finance, she is one of the first women to be CFO of such a large institution. At the University, she has been the highest-ranking woman administrator. She has been much in demand off-campus, serving as trustee or consultant to a wide range of educational institutions and business operations and as the first woman president of the National Association of College and University Business Officers.

Mary Lai learned to handle responsibilities early. At the age of 10 she began helping her parents run the family grocery store in the Greenpoint section of Brooklyn. She also looked after two younger brothers and a sister. At LIU on scholarship she held almost every major student office, won countless awards for scholastic achievement and service and was Queen of the Varsity Ball. Not so incidentally, at LIU she met her husband to be, the athletic and scholarly William T. "Buck" Lai B'41, who was to become the University's athletic director.

Mary Lai stresses a point to Chancellor Albert Bush-Brown, who appears skeptical of her input.

Her day-by-day responsibilities include supervision of all financial operations, long-range financial and physical planning, construction and maintenance programs at the various campuses and University investments. LIU was small and struggling in 1946 when Mary Lai accepted her bursar's job. Today it is the eighth largest private university in the United States. Mary Lai has gone the distance through crisis, expansion, economic ups and downs. When the situation has demanded she has been rigorously frugal with her budget or expansively generous with her donations.

When the University's finance building was named in her honor in 1996, President Steinberg reminded all present that "Faith, family and finances are the three pillars of Mary Lai's life…" Today, she projects a vitality that is not a whit diminished from the old days in the crowded streets of downtown Brooklyn. In Mary Lai, the spirit of '46 and of Long Island University is alive and thriving.

— From an article by Len Karlin B'47 in Long Island University Magazine, May, 1996. Karlin was assistant to the president, and head of public relations and publications for the University from 1950 to 1965.

"Buck" and Mary Lai.

Memories

Fred W. Thiele Jr. S'76, H'01 is now a New York State assemblyman representing Suffolk County's Second District.

One of the University's most prominent alums, the late Rose Bird B'58 (center), was the first woman to serve on California's Supreme Court. A scholarship student, Bird was a controversial figure in California for her pioneering commitments to strengthening environmental laws and consumer rights, and for her opposition to the death penalty.

Time-Life photographer Paul Schutzer B'52 (shown in top photo receiving an award from President Eisenhower) recorded signal moments in world history, from combat in the mid- and far east to presidential successions in this country. Shown is Schutzer's memorable photograph for Life Magazine which captured all the hope and promise of the new Kennedy administration. His career was cut short when he was killed on assignment covering the Mideast war in June 1967. He was out front, riding a halftrack, standing up and taking pictures.

Pulitzer Prize-winning author and columnist Jimmy Breslin B'51 ranks among the most illustrious alumni of the Brooklyn Campus. His latest book, "I Don't Want to Go to Jail," was published by Little Brown in 2001.

When the University needed the right man for a crucial time it often turned to William T. "Buck" Lai B'41. In 1951, he stepped up to become Brooklyn's director of athletics when Clair Bee stepped down after the basketball scandals. When basketball was reinstated in 1956, he created Operation Rebound, coaching a team of mostly green players to a 12-6 season ("We surprised everybody!"). He chaired Brooklyn's Physical Education Department, wrote how-to sports books, helped plan athletic facilities (including the transformation of the Paramount Theater into Brooklyn's gym) and launched the program for handicapped students. In the turmoil of the late 60's he served as Brooklyn's acting provost, handling one confrontation with angry students with calm understanding and lunch at Junior's. Buck is pictured here with two of the University's other stars — the chief financial officer (and his wife), Mary M. Lai B'42, H'86, and retired coach Clair Bee.

It's hard to avoid the cliché "Renaissance man" when describing Professor Nathan Resnick B'33. At the Brooklyn Campus for 40 years, he was a musician, artist, scholar, naturalist, writer, specialist on Walt Whitman — and that was in his spare time. Officially, he was director of libraries, chairman of the art department, director of the University Press, director of exhibitions, campus planner, dean for development of Learning Center programs and member of numerous faculty committees. In 1969, Professor Resnick was honored as "Alumnus of the Year." It was a tribute to "his outstanding service to the University and his leadership in the fight to save the Brooklyn Center." There was a lot going on under that hat.

"What we had here was a time and place in history. ... I'd stack up the education we got against any university on the face of the earth."

— Ruth Cummings P'60

CHAPTER FIVE
STUDENT LIFE

Suits and ties were standard garb for male collegians like these pharmacy students at Brooklyn. Above: Professor Otto Ruhmer amplified the importance of history in between chemistry courses.

Social Hour, Long Island University

Let's hear it for Brooklyn!

Truth, Independence, Efficiency . . . Ultimately, they belong so close together that each helps to make the other real. The seeker after truth is likely also to be the one who is independent, critical, courageous. But he is able to seek truth hopefully if he is trained well in the technique of the art or science that stirs his enthusiasm. As a student, he is most likely to develop these attributes if he belongs to a college that is not indifferent to the individual, not so large that its routines are mechanical, and yet large enough to afford him the values of modern equipment, multiple activities, personal associations with student and faculty.

To the extent, then, to which a college enables you to approach these ideals will it prepare you for successful living in a social world rich with promise and adventure.

If Long Island University, young, spirited, yet matured by several years of rigorous experience, seems to you to offer such opportunity, then we should like to know you. We are particularly and sincerely interested in you because, through your attention to this booklet, you have shown in turn an interest in what we hold to be of great importance to the young man or woman of today: the challenge of our changing world.

Long Island University

The Brooklyn Campus' gymnasium takes shape on what had been the orchestra floor of the fabled Paramount Theater. Shown are the athletic director at the time, William "Buck" Lai (left), and basketball coach Roy Rubin.

Men's basketball at a high level is a decades-long tradition — the program soared to the 1,000th victory mark in 2001. The proud Blackbird history includes qualifying for three Division I NCAA tournaments, capturing two N.I.T. championships and racking up two undefeated seasons.

Football has been the cornerstone of the C.W. Post Pioneer athletic program since its inception in 1957.

Southampton students maintained their own firefighting brigade. In 1967, they battled a brush fire that threatened the perimeter of the campus.

Opposing teams saw double trouble when the Breivaite twins took to the court. Rita and Evelyna Breivaite S'00 of Panavezys, Lithuania, came to Southampton in 1996 and from their freshman year were twin stars on the Lady Colonials. They were matching achievers in the classroom too, graduating cum laude and cum laude respectively.

LONG ISLAND UNIVERSITY
Department of Music

HOLIDAY CONCERT

The Long Island University Choral Society

Martin D. Josman, Director

Sunday Afternoon, December 16, 1956 - 3 P.M.

Carnegie Recital Hall

From classical to rock, music has always been a part of memorable University events. Here, a Brooklyn ensemble concentrates on performing in no less than Carnegie Recital Hall.

University musicians have the brass to toot their own horns.

LONG ISLAND UNIVERSITY

HOLIDAY CONCERT

- L.I.U. Community Choral Society
- L.I.U. Singers
- L.I.U. Band

DIRECTION
William T. Eicher
Band

Martin D. Josman
Choral Society and Singers

**Carnegie Recital Hall
Fri. Eve., Dec. 16, 1955**

Admission $1.80 — All Seats Reserved
Tickets on Sale at Bursar's Office
Send Checks or Money Orders to:
Department of Music
Long Island University
Brooklyn 1, New York

Memories

The lure of land, sea and air

I came to Southampton to study Marine Science and then decided to broaden my scope to include the whole environment which is so beautiful and diverse there. I remember how much of school life revolved around the environment — not only field biology, marine biology and the chance to work with environmental agencies, but just walking to class on a golden autumn day, the blue bay shimmering in the distance.

— Farrell Hochmuth S'97
Fulbright Scholar

Tom Petty (shown above), Crosby, Stills & Nash, Jimmy Buffet, Paul Simon, James Taylor and Tina Turner are among the musical legends that have rocked Southampton to raise money for marine and environmental science scholarships. All for the Sea, the annual benefit concert that draws these headliners to campus, was dubbed "the East End's biggest event of the summer" by Newsday; it has raised over $7 million since its inception in 1992. Inset: Students, alumni and local residents join together to support the College while sharing an evening of music under the stars.

*I made the train.
I got a spot!*

Jumping the hurdles at C.W. Post.

Student Union.

Post students time travel back a few centuries to joust at the annual Renaissance Fair. Shown are two 1982 knights battling for a fair lady's hand.

In 1943, members of Brooklyn's Folk Dance Club, in dirndles, prepare for a traditional dance.

In a league of their own, the C.W. Post women's softball team became a formidable competitor in the '80s.

Were you there when Southampton took the top prize? Shown is Southampton's championship lacrosse team, winner of the 1984 Knickerbocker Conference.

Good taste and modesty were once mandatory for C.W. Post coeds. These campus rules for women were issued during the 1966-67 school year.

Women's Residence Handbook

C. W. POST COLLEGE

1966-1967

College women are not permitted to wear slacks or shorts on campus and in all college buildings including the Library and Dining Hall.

Bermudas and slacks may be worn *in* the Residence Halls, except in the Main Lounges, during the day. After 6:00 P.M., on weekdays (Mon.-Thurs.), they may be worn on campus with the exception of the Library. On weekends this apparel is appropriate except when going to the Library or the Dining Hall.

Skirts are worn to all meals except Sunday dinner, at which time dresses or suits, stockings and heels are appropriate. Sneakers *may not* be worn in the Dining Hall at any evening meal or on Sunday.

Hair curlers *may not* be worn in the Main Lounges of the Residence Halls, or anywhere on campus.

Suitable covering, e.g.; a trench coat, must be worn to and from the swimming pool.

For physical education the attire that is called for will be worn.

On public conveyances, students are expected to wear dresses or suits.

Students are required to wear skirts off campus for *any event*, except when going directly to the beach or a friend's house.

(6)

Heiress Marjorie Merriweather Post, whose Long Island home is now the centerpiece of the C.W. Post Campus, meets with an early '60s student group to share stories about the Campus' fabulous Gold Coast history.

Paging Women

Coeds Have Weekend to Remember

By Anne Hannan

Mrs. Herbert May (Marjorie Merriweather Post), queenliest of Washington's glamorous hostesses, played fairy godmother this weekend to 22 coeds from C. W. Post College in Brookville.

Fairy godmothers don't wave wands these days, but to the girls, all members of the college's Sigma Alpha Theta Sorority, Mrs. May fills the bill in every other way. An honorary member of their sorority, the fabled Mrs. May, heiress to the Post Toastie fortune and one-time wife of the late Joseph P. Davies, former U.S. ambassador to Russia, thought it would be nice if her sorority "sisters" could see the nation's capitol. So, with a gracious invitation to come to Washington, she provided the girls with a trip that was both educational and " a little fun, too."

She chose a time when Washington was at its fairyland loveliest—the weekend of the Cherry-Blossom Festival and even though the blossoms were not out, the girls thought the city beautiful.

She arranged for a special tour of the White House after the tourists had left on Saturday, along with visits to Mount Vernon, Arlington Cemetery and other historical points in the city.

She provided a modern magic carpet to carry the girls, and their chaperones away for the weekend—her own private turbo-prop Viscount, the Merriweather.

And she lined up 22 Prince Charmings as escorts for the college students during an evening of dinner and dancing in an exclusive Washington Hotel.

Back to earth Sunday night, Barbara Reed of Glen Cove, one the lucky 22, breathlessly described the trip as "wonderful, just grand, a taste of another world."

"She did everything so beautifully," the college junior said. "She was so graceful, it reminded me of a queen in her palace. But no one was shy with Mrs. May. She's well, so down to earth, too."

The girls were guests of Mrs. May for luncheon Saturday and again Sunday at Hillwood, the May home in Washington, which "took my breath away, it was so beautiful," Miss Reed said.

The visit to the White House included a few minutes in President Eisenhower's private quarters (though the girls did not meet him) and a quick look into the room where the Cabinet meets. "It smelled like cigar smoke and leather," according to Miss Reed, and the girls also left feeling a little closer to history-in-the-making.

The evening was one to set college girls dreaming of best dresses, champagne and flowers. They dressed "to the hilt," pinned on the camellias Mr. and Mrs. May had sent each one and went off to be wined and dined.

Their escorts, whom they met at a pre-dinner cocktail party at Hillwood, were picked from a list of eligible Washington bachelors by Mrs. May.

"If she wanted us to really feel part of everything going on in Washington she couldn't have found a better way," Miss Reed said. "The men were all involved in government; they seemed to know all about everything. We all talked and talked."

Home by 12:30, the girls slept very little, talking until dawn and then getting ready for a trip to mount Vernon and a final luncheon with their hostess and her husband.

The girls are back in class today, their gowns packed away and their camellia corsages pressed into memory books. But if they have a little difficulty concentrating on lessons, who can blame them? In the Atomic Age, not every girl has a fairy godmother, even for one weekend.

ON THE TOWN in Washington this weekend were girls from C. W. Post College, two of whom are shown above with their escorts and their hostess, Mrs. Herbert May (Marjorie Merriweather Post), left. Others, from left, are John F. Simmons, Washington, Barbara Bayne, East Northport, Barbara Reed, Glen Cove, and George M. Ferris Jr., Washington, in Mrs. May's home, Hillwood, at party before dinner-dance in hotel. (UPI Telephoto)

AT WHITE HOUSE for special tour are Barbara Reed, right, and Mrs. R. Gordon Hoxie, wife of dean of college, who accompanied girls. (AP Photo)

TESTING the bunk beds in the Merriweather, Mrs. May's private plane, is Martha Furno, Smithtown, while Suzanne Donohue, Rockville Centre, watches. (Newsday Photo by De Bear)

FOR THE SCRAPBOOK, one picture. Patricia Doran, Huntington, and Trudy Melsom, Little neck, pose in front of plane. Barbara Reed, Glen Cove, snaps them. (Newsday Photo by De Bear)

Monday, April 11, 1960

A 1960 C.W. posting to Washington, D.C.

The members of the 1966 C.W. Post crew achieved their championship status with regular practice sessions on the waters of nearby Long Island Sound.

Coach Buck Lai points the way toward a winning basketball match for his '57 Blackbirds.

With unwavering belief in his young men from the playing fields of Brooklyn, Professor Arthur Yates, founder of the Long Island University Rugby Club, coached the team onward and upward to a top place in the intercollegiate standings—right up there with Harvard and Yale.

William "Dolly" King played basketball and football for Long Island University from 1937 to 1941. A plaque on the Wall of Fame in Brooklyn's Founders Hall reads: "He was captain of the football team who played offensive end for the Blackbirds on Thanksgiving day in 1939, and then played 40 minutes of basketball at Madison Square Garden that night. He was the greatest all-around athlete in school history."

"King-Pin"

We are proud to dedicate this section of our year book to "Dolly" King—the outstanding player of the year—outstanding not only in athletic ability but also in sportsmanship and clean play.

131

Go Team!

Student newspapers

Brooklyn

Southampton

C.W. Post

A Friends World student climbs the ancient hills of Jordan.

From musical comedy to Shakespearean tragedy, from the cutting edge to the classic, the theater is a vibrant tradition at all Long Island University campuses. Brooklyn, long the scene of popular hits, is now known for its flair for the experimental and will soon receive a new theater donated by trustee Steven Kumble and his wife, Peggy. Post's profusion of theater productions include "The Skriker," selected to perform at Kennedy Center in Washington, D.C. in 1998. The Southampton Players regularly present ambitious dramas and musicals to full houses and fine reviews at Southampton College. The University may well claim (in Milton's phrase) "the well-trod stage."

Memories

The grip of friendship

One of my favorite memories is from my freshman year, actually my first day. I had already met my roommate, Ardis Thompson, and we met our suite mates and the rest of our freshman group. And we did our little group activities where you wrap yourselves into those huge human knots and then untangle yourselves. I kept taking one person's hand, Michelle Sickels' (now the mother of a four-year-old girl), and I haven't let go. We are still the best of friends.

— Vicki Guarrascino S'95

Touch football supplements an array of organized sports at Southampton College.

Taking strides at Southampton College means more than learning to traverse the campus's 110 rolling acres.

Early Southampton students enjoy a dining hall that retains the tranquility of its gracious past. Today, the renovated space serves as Southampton College's registrar's office.

Memories

"Play with the Bunnies"

Southampton College had a campaign for the Heart Fund called "Bounce for Beats." People would donate money for a bounce-the-basketball contest. We decided to do something different. Instead of "Bounce for Beats" we decided on "Play with the Bunnies." So we had this big campaign in the community whereby anybody in town who paid $50 a minute got to play in the basketball game with the Playboy bunnies. Of course, the Playboy bunnies were a big deal in those days; the Playboy Club was very hot. And it was every man's fantasy to play with the bunnies. We had a motorcade in town; someone paid to be referee and another to be team doctor. It was a catch-as-catch-can game, very casual. We had a great turnout; it was very successful and it was a lot of fun.

— Alan Braveman S'68

C.W. Post's men's lacrosse team has been a force to be reckoned with in Division II, making the NCAA tournament five times in six years (1996-2001) and capturing the national championship in 1996.

C.W. Post teamwork.

THE TOP TEN REASONS TO GO TO LIU/SOUTHAMPTON CAMPUS

10 - PUBLIC SAFETY??
9 - PLANET BANANA FISH??!!
8 - LUXURY ROOMS WITH CABLE T.V.
7 - GOURMET FOOD SERVICES.
6 - THURSDAY AT DANNY'S "BEAT THE CLOCK" NIGHT.
5 - THE ALL STAR FOOTBALL TEAM.
4 - UNLIMITED FREE PARKING.
3 - ALL NEW SAUNA AND EXERCISE ROOM.
2 - SMALL ENOUGH TO MINGLE-BIG ENOUGH TO SCORE.
1 - I HAD NOTHING BETTER TO DO WITH $65,640

Students love Southampton College for many reasons. This may be one of them.

Memories

Clair Bee — a coach for all seasons

He was known as "Mr. Basketball." He was one of the great teachers of the game, the conceptual basketball genius of his day, a coach respected and feared by every major college basketball team, an author of sports novels for young people and of how-to-play-the-game books, a humorous, charismatic public speaker, a man whose accomplishments are listed in the Naismith Basketball Hall of Fame, a man who became an LIU legend.

In 1932, he took over the reins as LIU basketball coach and in a dilapidated church gymnasium in Brooklyn shaped a winning team, guiding it through its glory days. In 1939, Bee's Blackbirds won the National Invitational Tournament, an exhilaratingly prestigious crown for such a small school. In 1941, LIU won its second N.I.T and in five other appearances the Blackbirds advanced to the quarterfinals. After the war, Bee's men set out on an even tougher schedule and gathered an enviable record. In 1950, the team went 20-4 playing the best teams in the country.

All of the above are why the 1951 point-shaving scandal, in which seven colleges were involved, hit LIU extra hard. It took down team and coach: LIU dropped its basketball program for six years; Clair Bee, no longer coach, became an administrator at the University and concentrated on his basketball camps. It was not till 1957, under the direction of William "Buck" Lai, a Bee protégé, that LIU returned to basketball with "Operation Rebound."

Clair Bee eventually went on to coach the Baltimore Bullets professional basketball team in the early days of the NBA. He retired to his upper New York State farm, becoming totally blind in the last years of his life. He died in 1983 and is still revered by those of us who knew him and by those who only know of him.

Excerpted from "Glory Days" by James B. Dolkas B'56

Bee and White reunion

There had been rumors that the boys on the basketball team might be shaving points for professional gamblers. Then, at 2 a.m. on February 14, 1951, in my role as LIU public relations director I got a phone call from the D.A.'s office. The boys had confessed. President Metcalfe, Buck Lai and I went down to 100 Center Street to Lt. Graffnecker's office to see if they needed an attorney. They did; eventually they were convicted.

After the point-shaving scandal lives were changed. Although he continued to be associated with LIU and with basketball camps, Clair Bee never coached LIU basketball again. Sherman White, who was probably the most promising player on the team, with a pro offer in his future, never realized that dream.

Years later, at a reunion honoring Clair Bee that turned out to be his last, many of his old players and many nationally known basketball players came to pay their respects to "Mr. Basketball." Bee, who was old and frail and almost blind, sat at the dais where he greeted a procession of men from his past. The door opened and a tall, majestic black man strode down to the dais. All he said was, "It's me, coach," and Bee knew, and they embraced. It was Sherman White.

— Len Karlin B'47

Despite the political turbulence of the '60s, Brooklyn Campus students still came out for basketball.

C. W. POST COLLEGE
Brookville, Long Island

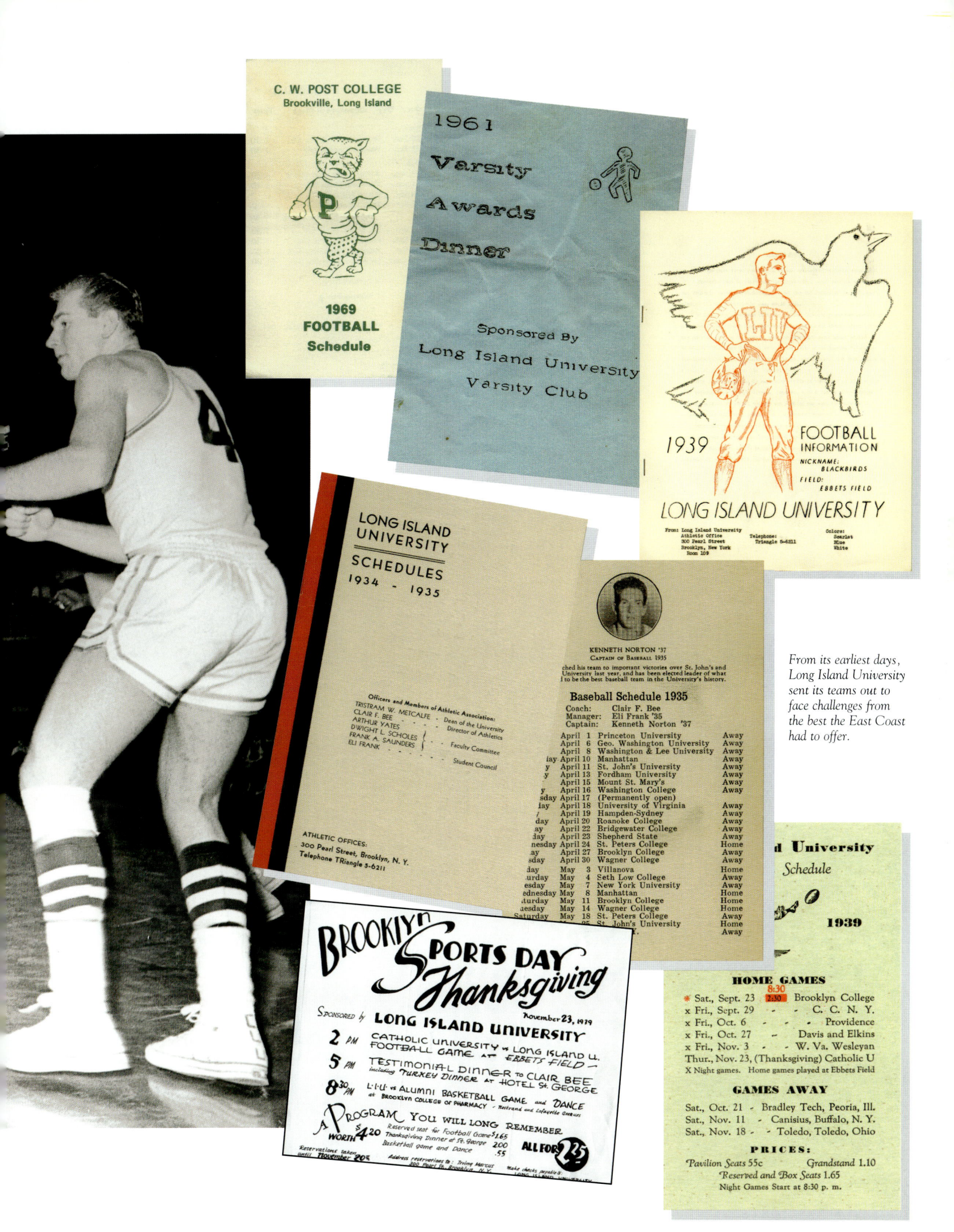

1969 FOOTBALL Schedule

1961 Varsity Awards Dinner

Sponsored By Long Island University Varsity Club

1939 FOOTBALL INFORMATION
NICKNAME: BLACKBIRDS
FIELD: EBBETS FIELD

LONG ISLAND UNIVERSITY

From: Long Island University
Athletic Office
300 Pearl Street
Brooklyn, New York
Room 109

Telephone: Triangle 5-6211

Colors: Scarlet Blue White

LONG ISLAND UNIVERSITY SCHEDULES 1934 - 1935

Officers and Members of Athletic Association:
TRISTRAM W. METCALFE — Dean of the University
CLAIR F. BEE — Director of Athletics
ARTHUR YATES
DWIGHT L. SCHOLES — Faculty Committee
FRANK A. SAUNDERS
ELI FRANK — Student Council

ATHLETIC OFFICES:
300 Pearl Street, Brooklyn, N. Y.
Telephone TRiangle 5-6211

KENNETH NORTON '37
CAPTAIN of BASEBALL 1935

coached his team to important victories over St. John's and
University last year, and has been elected leader of what
to be the best baseball team in the University's history.

Baseball Schedule 1935
Coach: Clair F. Bee
Manager: Eli Frank '35
Captain: Kenneth Norton '37

April 1	Princeton University	Away
April 6	Geo. Washington University	Away
April 8	Washington & Lee University	Away
April 10	Manhattan	Away
April 11	St. John's University	Away
April 13	Fordham University	Away
April 15	Mount St. Mary's	Away
April 16	Washington College	Away
April 17	(Permanently open)	
April 18	University of Virginia	Away
April 19	Hampden-Sydney	Away
April 20	Roanoke College	Away
April 22	Bridgewater College	Away
April 23	Shepherd State	Away
April 24	St. Peters College	Home
April 27	Brooklyn College	Away
April 30	Wagner College	Away
May 3	Villanova	Home
May 4	Seth Low College	Away
May 7	New York University	Away
May 8	Manhattan	Home
May 11	Brooklyn College	Home
May 14	Wagner College	Home
May 18	St. Peters College	Away
	St. John's University	Home
		Away

Brooklyn SPORTS DAY Thanksgiving
November 23, 1939
Sponsored by LONG ISLAND UNIVERSITY

2 PM CATHOLIC UNIVERSITY vs LONG ISLAND U. FOOTBALL GAME at EBBETS FIELD
5 PM TESTIMONIAL DINNER to CLAIR BEE including TURKEY DINNER at HOTEL ST. GEORGE
8:30 PM L·I·U· vs ALUMNI BASKETBALL GAME and DANCE at BROOKLYN COLLEGE of PHARMACY - Nostrand and Lafayette Avenues

A PROGRAM YOU WILL LONG REMEMBER

WORTH $4.20
Reserved seat for Football Game $1.65
Thanksgiving Dinner at St. George 2.00
Basketball game and Dance .55

ALL FOR $2.25

Reservations taken until November 20th
Address reservations to: Irving Marcus
300 Pearl St. Brooklyn, N.Y.
Make checks payable to LONG ISLAND UNIVERSITY

From its earliest days, Long Island University sent its teams out to face challenges from the best the East Coast had to offer.

Long Island University Schedule 1939

HOME GAMES
* Sat., Sept. 23 8:30 Brooklyn College 2:30
x Fri., Sept. 29 — C.C.N.Y.
x Fri., Oct. 6 — Providence
x Fri., Oct. 27 — Davis and Elkins
x Fri., Nov. 3 — W. Va. Wesleyan
Thur., Nov. 23, (Thanksgiving) Catholic U
X Night games. Home games played at Ebbets Field

GAMES AWAY
Sat., Oct. 21 - Bradley Tech, Peoria, Ill.
Sat., Nov. 11 - Canisius, Buffalo, N.Y.
Sat., Nov. 18 - Toledo, Toledo, Ohio

PRICES:
Pavilion Seats 55c   Grandstand 1.10
Reserved and Box Seats 1.65
Night Games Start at 8:30 p.m.

The sweethearts of Sigma Alpha Theta reminisce...

Memories

The first Blue Christmas Ball, 1965. It was held in the Great Hall. The women wore white or blue. I'll never forget the silver ball with many facets that hung from the ceiling and it turned and turned and there was starlight all over the room

— Barbara Bane Ohlig P'59

It was a marvelous time and we loved it. We had a very unique opportunity here. What we had here was a time and place in history. Very unique. I would stack up the education we got — not just in the classroom but in doing a lot of extracurricular things because we were forming organizations, creating traditions — I'd stack up the education we got against any university on the face of the earth.

— Ruth Cummings, P'60

Up above the fireplace in the Great Hall: Mens regnum bona possidet. "A good mind possesses a kingdom." Dr. Meiselman, you started me on the way to that. The rest of the people I met at Post continued me on that path. Today I know I was very lucky.

— Nina Panaseny Anastasio, P'66, (M.S.)'70

Memories

Turbulent Times

I think part of what gave us our giddiness or existential ecstasy (for lack of a better term) was the serious stuff that was going on around us — the assassination of President Kennedy, the shooting by Jack Ruby (I was sitting at my T.V. and was rocked to the nth degree), the Bobby Kennedy assassination. Then, when Martin Luther King was killed, it was very frightening. I remember coming home and thinking there would be riots and the world would come to an end. It was such a monumental moment in everybody's lives. I think the times might have been the reason for a lot of the hijinks and devil-may-care attitude. Nobody worried about tomorrow. It was a live for today philosophy.

— Alan Braveman S'68

A Vietnam-era war protest poster and a beloved childhood doll coexist peacefully in a Southampton dorm room, circa 1970.

Finals week.

C.W. Post coed takes a break, '60s style.

A Note on Sources for "A History"

In writing our account of Long Island University we were helped by many people and drew upon many sources. One major history, to which we give the reference in our first textual footnote, was written by Elliott S. M. Gatner, a librarian and full professor at Brooklyn, whose involvement in university-wide matters and careful research enabled him to give a detailed account of the years up to 1968 that is remarkably neutral on controversial issues. A smaller, but also useful history, was written by Leonard Karlin, former assistant to the president and head of public relations and publications for the University. The University-published volume, "Preface to the Future," 1967, gives an account of President Hoxie's plans for a graduate university.

Together and separately, we conducted, on the separate campuses, formal interviews of one to three hours with 16 people from among the faculty, administrators and staff. Working among interested participants in the University's history, we talked with many others, including students. We also interviewed President Steinberg. It was Dr. Steinberg who requested that we write this essay and who insisted that it reflect our independent judgement as scholars. Members of our 25 person advisory panel, consisting of faculty, staff and administrators from all over the University, commented on our early plans, sent us memories throughout the months when we were doing the research and read the manuscript with critical and constructive eyes. These and many other people gave us the contents of their personal files. The archivists at Brooklyn, C.W. Post, and especially Janet F. Marks at University Center, provided much documentary material. Their and other people's contributions have included clippings, photocopies of early documents, copies of the statutes, lists of board members, organizational charts, Middle States reports, annual financial reports, and copies of the campus newspapers, University bulletins, alumni publications, brochures, and ephemeral newsletters.

To put this material in context, we gathered background information in three other areas: higher education in general, as well as in the New York and Long Island regions; the outside people who have contributed to its growth; and the local and national history of the times.

We thank the many people who generously gave us their time, their written materials, their confidence, and their enthusiasm — all of which we hope we have held in trust.

— Maren Lockwood Carden, Ph.D.
Susan E. Dinan, Ph.D.

---

[1] Elliott S. M. Gatner, Long Island: The History of a Relevant and Responsive University, 1926-1968. Columbia University, Ed.D., 1975, 72. Many of the details about the University's early growth come from this work. For details on how we gathered material for this research see Note on Sources above.
[2] Gatner, 24
[3] Before it moved to the Paramount building in 1950 the University's other official addresses that were rented and used for shorter periods included two other buildings on Pearl Street and its very first home on Court Street.
[4] Recollections of Lillian Huriash Benowitz B'31.
[5] Letter, Adeline K. Kerlin to Miss McCullum, December 1, 1931.
[6] Letter, George R. Hardie to Mrs. Robert T. Kerlin, May 8, 1929.
[7] Long Island University Fiftieth Anniversary Celebration, brochure.
[8] Quoted in Gatner, 111.
[9] Gatner, 204
[10] Gatner, 117
[11] Recollection of Leonard Karlin, former assistant to the president and head of public relations and publications for the University, 2001.
[12] Gatner, 139.
[13] Gatner, 244
[14] Report to the Board of Trustees, n.d.
[15] Dean Hugo H. Schaefer, quoted in Gatner, 512.
[16] Gatner, 301.
[17] Gatner, 323-5
[18] Long Island University, Preface to the Future: The Ten-Year Plan of Long Island University. Greenvale, NY: Long Island University, 1967.
[19] Lapel buttons said, "Huck Foxie."
[20] Some faculty members, like Nathan Resnick, worked primarily behind the scenes but most made very visible protests.
[21] New York State Joint Legislature Committee on Higher Education. Special interim report of the Joint Legislative Committee on Higher Education, Nov. 30, 1967, 80. Quoted in Gatner, 485.
[22] Special Interim Report, 46. In Gatner, 488.
[23] Median family incomes at the Brooklyn and Southampton Campuses are less than the U.S. median. At C.W. Post, the median is about $10,000 above the U.S. median. From University "Profile" and U.S. population data in The World Almanac, 2000.
[24] Chronicle of Higher Education, Oct 27, 2000, loans now the primary source of student aid. Fifty-nine percent from loans. In 1980, 41 percent came from loans.
[25] Letter, David J. Steinberg to Congressman Peter T. King, December 19, 1995.
[26] Middle States, "University Wide Report," 1993.
[27] Middle States, "University Wide Report," 1993.

HISTORY ADVISORY BOARD

Anne Burns P'70, (M.S.) '71
Alan Chaves
Arthur Colemam
William F. de Neergaard Ph'47
Alexander Dashnaw
Carol Gilbert
Lewis Greenstein
Thomas Haresign

Len Karlin B'47
Mary Lai B'41, H'86
Newton Meiselman
Bob Pavese P'74
William Peterson
Vince Salamone P'64
Joan Shields
Steven Straus

John Strong
Harry Stucke
George Sutton
Matilda Tazzi
Mary Topping
Martin Tucker
Don Ungarelli P'60, (M.S.) '62

ACKNOWLEDGEMENTS

Nina Panaseny Anastasio P'66, (M.S.) '70
Kenneth Anderson
Murray Bach S'84
Bachrach Photographers
Stanley Barshay P'60
Jerry Bauer
Ellen Belcher
Ben Benowitz
Lillian Huriash Benowitz B'31
Brian Merlis Collection
   (photo by Robert Presbrey)
Alan Braveman S'68
Bush-Brown Archives
Frances Bush-Brown
Daniel Chapman B'40
Cox Black and White Lab, Inc.
Patricia Gilroy Crowe P'59
Ruth Cummings P'60
Debra Curtis P'82
Cynthia Dantzig
James B. Dolkas B'56
John Doria B'57
Jane Finalborgo
Jodie Fine P'73
Fotomasters
Greg Fox
Joan Geluso Franzone P'64
Robert Gerbereux
Vicki Guarascino S'95

Romy Haller P'96, (M.S.) '00
Patricia Doran Hallinan P'61
Helen Hammond
Joan Harrison
James M. Hester
Charles Hitchcock
Sally L'Ecuyer Hogeman P'62
I.C.A. Photographers
Island Metro Publications
Darren Johnson S'92
Joanne Hocker Kirchner P'63
William "Buck" Lai B'41
Rita Langdon P'91, (M.A.) '95
Arthur Leipzig
Mimi Leipzig
Cynthia Lenox P'63
Pamela Lennox
George LoPresti B'61
Sue Donohue Mackenzie P'59
Carl O. Mamay
Melinda Marino P'00
Virginia Marshall P'63, (M.S.) '67
Julian Mates
Annette McCarthy S'96
Toni Anastasio McKeen P'65, (M.S.) '69
Kenneth Mensing
Kurt J. Metzdorf (Print by Haig Shekerjian)
Lloyd Newman B'52

Phyllis Neuman S'80
Sidney Offit H'99
Barbara Bane Ohlig P'59
Lynn O'Pasek
Barbara Pasternak
Jill E. Pisciotta S'90
William Roberson,
   Rogers Memorial Library,
   Southampton
Charles W. Rohrer B'56
Helen Saffran
Jane Donnelly Schmitt P'60, (M.S.) '64
Conrad Schoeffling P'77
Gladys Schrynemakers
Anneliese Schumacher
Barbara Reed Smith
Southampton Press
Diana Spirt P'59, (M.S.) '61
John Strong
Brad Sullivan
Henry Suydam, Life Magazine
Mary Topping
Allison Towle S'98
Jane Trotto
Van Burgess
Chris Vultaggio P'99
Jacqueline Barrie Wallace P'63
Constance Woo P'95 (M.S.)

PHOTO CREDITS

FRONT MATTER

The Brooklyn Bridge - September 11, 2001, Michelle Agins/NYT Pictures

p. 1	from left to right: Frank Harmon; UA; Ralph O. Gottlob, B'49; UA
p. 3	Gina Motisi

CAMPUSES

p. 5	from left to right: UA; Mark McQueen; Mark McQueen; Mark McQueen
p. 6	Mark McQueen
p. 7	Mark McQueen
p. 8-9	Mark McQueen
p. 10	Don Hamerman
p. 11	Brian Ballweg
p. 13	(top) Mark McQueen; (bottom) Bruce Bennett Studios
p. 14	Rodney K. Hurley B'87
p. 16	Mark McQueen
p. 17	(top) Stephen Hausler
p. 18	Mark McQueen
p. 19	Anita Filippi-D'Anca
p. 20	Mark McQueen
p. 22	(top) Ray O'Connor; (bottom) Mark McQueen
p. 23	Mark McQueen
p. 24	Mark McQueen

INTELLECTUAL LIFE

p. 27	UA; Mark McQueen; UA; UA
p. 30	(inset) Bruce Bennett Studios
p. 31	Gary J. Mamay
p. 33	(center) Sally Mueller B'85
p. 34	Mark McQueen
p. 36	Edward J. Edahl
p. 37	(bottom) Davis A. Gaffga
p. 39	Bachrach
p. 40	Mark McQueen
p. 42	Pioneer
p. 43	Mark McQueen
p. 44	(top) Pioneer
p. 45	Rita Langdon P'91, (M.A.) '95
p. 47	Arthur Studios Inc.
p. 48	Mark McQueen; (inset) UA
p. 49	Mark McQueen
p. 51	(left) courtesy of The New York Times
p. 52	Mark McQueen

HISTORY

p. 61	(top) Royal Photo Studio; (bottom) Brooklyn Public Library-Brooklyn Collection
p. 64-65	Cliff DeBear, Newsday
p. 65	(right) Brian Merlis Collection, photo by Robert Presbrey
p. 68	Gina Motisi
p. 73	(left) Kenneth Sanderson; (bottom) Pioneer
p. 82	(top) Pioneer
p. 83	Gina Motisi
p. 87	Rodney K. Hurley B'87

Images for global events in the timeline provided by Corbis.

PERSONALITIES

p. 93	from left to right: UA; Navy Dept., National Archives; UA; Luigi Pelettieri
p. 94	(bottom right) Ralph O. Gottlob B'49
p. 97	(top) Bruce Bennett Studios
p. 98	(left) Luigi Pelettieri
p. 98-99	Navy Dept., National Archives
p. 100	(top) Rodney K. Hurley B'87
p. 103	(top left) Barbara Frohman P'94, (M.F.A.) '96; (top right) Gordon Grant; (bottom left) courtesy of Mr. and Mrs. Winnick; (bottom right) Mark McQueen
p. 106	(bottom) Bruce Bennett Studios
p. 108	(top) Gary J. Mamay; (bottom) California History Room, California State Library
p. 109	Paul Schutzer B'52/Timepix; (inset) Robert Phillips/Timepix
p. 110	(top left) courtesy Little, Brown and Company

STUDENT LIFE

p. 113	(right) Rodney K. Hurley B'87
p. 115	(top) Rodney K. Hurley B'87
p. 117	(right) Gene Boyars
p. 118	Vincent Dusovic
p. 119	(bottom) Joe Dionisio
p. 122	Gary J. Mamay
p. 126	(bottom) Gene Pincus B'48
p. 128	Courtesy of Hillwood Museum and Gardens, Washington, D.C.
p. 136	David M. Krasnow S'82
p. 137	(top) David M. Krasnow S'82
p. 138	(right) Joe Rogate
p. 140	Mark McQueen
p. 147	courtesy of Virginia Marshall P'63, (M.S.)'67

COVERS

Inside front: Brooklyn Public Library - Brooklyn Collection
Inside back: Robert Lipper

All 3D objects were photographed by Mark McQueen with the exception of those appearing on pages 106, 130 and 131 which were shot by Rodney K. Hurley B'87.

Unless otherwise credited, all photos are from the Long Island University Archives.

The photo montage on the dust jacket includes works by some of the photographers listed above.

INDEX

A
Abruzzo, Mathew T., 63
Administration Building (C.W. Post). *See* Gary Winnick House
Administration Center, 72. *See also* Bush-Brown Hall
All for the Sea, 88, 103, **122**
Anastasio, Nina Panaseny P'66, 144
Arden, Eugene, 69
Arnold & Marie Schwartz College of Pharmacy and Health Sciences, **49, 58, 65, 66,** 67, 78, 83
Arthur T. Roth Graduate School of Business Administration, 73, 79. *See also* College of Management.

B
B. Davis Schwartz Memorial Library, **21**
Banks, Murray, 64
Barshay, Stanley P'60, 36
"Battle of Brookville," 57, 67, 68, 87
Bee, Clair F., 61, 66, 68, 71, **110, 141**
Belafonte, Harry, **100**
Benowitz, Lillian Huriash B'31, **41,** 60
Bird, Rose B'58, 61, **108**
Birenbaum, William M., 73-75, 78
Bishop, Timothy H., 91
Braveman, Alan, 138, 145
Breivaite, Rita and Evelyna S'00, **119**
Brentwood Campus, **15,** 57, 70, **75,** 83, 91
Breslin, Jimmy B'51, **110**
Brier, Bob, **40**
Brooklyn College of Pharmacy. *See* Arnold & Marie Schwartz College of Pharmacy and Health Sciences
Brooklyn Paramount Theater, **6,** 60, **65,** 71, 78, 116
Buffet, Jimmy, 122
Bush-Brown, Albert, **28-29,** 77-83, 88, **107**
Bush-Brown Hall, **77**

C
Cangero, Sylvester, 68, **96**
Carden, Maren Lockwood, 56
Chancellors Hall, **5, 20, 90**
Charles, Harold, 74
Childs, Theodore F., 75
Chu, Heting, **48**
civil rights movement. *See* Long Island University, civil rights movement
Clark, Edward A., 78
College of Management, 69
Conolly, Richard, 57, 68, 70, 72, 76, **93, 94, 99**
Cook, Edward J., 79
Crosby, Stills & Nash, 122
Cummings, Ruth P'60, 112, 144

D
Davies, Joseph, 68
Davis, Colonius, **37**
de Barritt, Mildred Loxtin Barritt, **39**
de Kooning, Willem, 71
de Neergaard, William, **106**
de Neergaard, William F., **106**
Dinan, Susan E., 56
disability rights movements. *See* LIU, disability rights
Dolkas, James B. B'56, 141
Doria, John L. B'57, **27, 30,** 64
Duke, Angier Biddle, **104**

E
E.R. Squibb and Sons. *See* Squibb, Edward Robinson
education
    and changes in, 85-87
    and establishment of a national movement in, 56-59
    impact from unions, strikes and protests, **55,** 73, 74, 81-83
    social responsibilities of students in, 61
Eisenhower, Dwight D., **109**
Eugene & Beverly Luntey Commons, **6**

F
federal legislation
    GI Bill of Rights, 57, 63-64, 69, 86
    Higher Education Acts of 1963, 74
    Morrill Acts of 1862, 58
    Pure Food and Drug Act of 1906, 66
Feiffer, Jules H'99, 38
Ferraru, Leon, **41**
Fitzgerald, F. Scott , 67
Fox, Mrs. William, 70
Freed, Allan, 65
Friends World Program, **25,** 57, 88, 87, 113, **134**

G
Gary Winnick House, **5, 7, 19,** 68, 87
Gatner, Elliott S.M., 59
Gershoy, Leo, 61, 92
George Polk Awards, **28-29,** 71, 79
GI Bill of Rights. *See* federal legislation, GI Bill of Rights
Glanz, Edward C., 71, 76
Greenstein, Lewis, 88
Graduate Library School, 48. *See also* Palmer School of Library and Information Science.
Gross, Stephen M., 87
Grossley, Richard P., 65
Guarrascino, Vicki, 136
Guirty, Geraldo B'45, 61

INDEX

H
Hardie, George Robert, 60
Harriman, Averill, **94**
Hawksworth, J.L., 99
Haynes, Gale Stevens, 90
Heilbrunn, Harriet B'32, 89, **103**
Heilbrunn, Robert, 89, **103**
Hester, James M., 99
Heumann, Judy B'69, H'94, 75, **97**.
   See also LIU, student disability movement
higher education. See education
Higher Education Acts of 1963. See federal legislation
Hillwood Commons auditorium. See Rose and
   Gilbert Tilles Center for the Performing Arts.
Hillwood mansion. See Gary Winnick House.
history
   of Long Island University, 56-91
Hitchcock, Chuck, 79
Hockmuth, Farrell S'97, **122**
Hoxie, R. Gordon, 70, 72-78, 79, 85, **94**
Hughes, Langston, **33**
Humphrey, Hubert H., **33**
Hutton, E.F., 68

I
immigration
   impact on University growth, 65
integration. See Long Island University, civil
   rights movement

J
Jeanette and Edmund T Pratt Jr. Center for
   Academic Studies, **14**, 87
Jeanette and Edmund T Pratt Jr. Recreation
   Center, **21**, 87
Johnson, Lyndon B., 86
Jonas, Ralph, 59

K
Kanas, John S'68, **102**
Kapatansky, Bernie, 63
Karlin, Len B'47, 107, 141
Kennedy, Jacqueline, **109**
Kennedy, John F., 75, **109**
Kennedy, Robert, 75
Kern, Rene, **50**
King, Peter T., 88
King, William "Dolly", 131
Knopf, Ralph, 75
Kumble, Steven, 135

L
Lafayette Avenue Building of Brooklyn
   College of Pharmacy, **66**, 78

L (continued)
Lai, Mary M., **3**, 63-64, **70**, 86, **102**, **107**, 110
Lai, William "Buck", 3, **70**, 74, **107**, 110, **116**, **130**, 141
LaMaccia, Armand, 72
Leipzig, Arthur, **51**
Lemberger, Louis, **105**
Lenox, Carleton, **37**
Lenox, Cynthia P'63, **37**
Library Learning Center, 78
Lindsay, John, **75**
Lipski, Donald, 88
LIU Plan, 86, 89
Long Island University
   1926 charter, **56**, 64
   and immigration, 59-60, 90
   and religion, 57-58
   and the Depression, 59-60
   and the military draft, 63
   approval of provisional charter for, 59
   campus life, **112-147**
   civil rights movement, 61, 65, 74-75
   establishment of University, 56-91
   financial support for, 56-57
   impact from the economy, 58-60, 64
   loss of enrollment, 63-64
   magazine, **38**
   mission of, 3, 60
   music, **120-21**
   Public Radio Network. See WPBX-FM.
   satellite programs, 70
   seal, 2
   sports, 61, 66-67, 69, 72, 113, 115, **117-19**, **124**, **127**,
      130-32, **138**, **141-43**
   student disability movement, 75, 78
Lorber Hall, **17**, 36
Luntey, Eugene H'98, **102**

M
MacArthur, Douglas, **33**
Marine Science, **1**, **43**, 71-72, 103, 122
Marmion, Harry A., 79
Mates, Julian, 44, 70
McGrath, John P., **93**, **94**, 98
McNeill, Don, **28-29**
Meiselman, Newton, **46**, 68
Metcalfe, Tristram Walker, 1, 3, **62-64**, 66
   72, **94**, 107
Middle States Association of Colleges and
   Secondary Schools, 4, 68, 85, 89, 91
Mitchel College, 70, 73
Mitchell, Morris, 88
Moore, Marianne, **33**
Morrill Acts of 1862. See federal legislation,
   Morrill Acts of 1862

152

INDEX

M *(continued)*
Moses, Robert, 67
Muhammed Ali, 75
Munford, Bob, 27, 44

N
New York State Board of Regents, 58, 59, 85
Neuman, Phyllis S'80, 80
Newman, Lloyd B'52, 35, 64
Newton, David, 83

O
Offit, Sidney, **28-29**
Ohlig, Barbara Bane P'59, 144

P
Palmer, Carleton, 37, 44, 69
Palmer, Winthrop, 37, 44, 69
Palmer School of Library and Information Science, **48**, 69, 73
Payton, Robert L., 76
Pell, John H. G., 71-72, **76**, 100
Perlman, Itzhak, **106**
Perlmutter, Emanuel, **32**
Petty, Tom, **122**
Pfeffer, Leo, 73
Pileggi, Nick B'56, 35
Pioneer, 76, 78, **133**
Polk Awards. *See* George Polk Awards.
Post, Charles William, **55**, **68**, **69**
Post, Marjorie Merriweather, **1**, **55**, 65, 68, 69, 72, 96, **128**
Pratt, Edmund T., **90**, **103**
Pratt, Jeanette, **90**, **103**
Pure Food and Drug Act of 1906. *See* federal legislation, Pure Food and Drug Act of 1906

Q
Quakers. *See* Society of Friends

R
Rather, Dan, **28-29**
Reisman, David, 57, 58
Reiss, Chester, 66
Resnick, Nathan B'33, **111**
Richardson, Lionel L., **93**, **101**
Roberts, Francis, **45**
Robinson, Jackie, **70**, 90
Rockefeller, Nelson A., 86
Rockland Graduate Campus, **16**, 57, 84, 91
Roosevelt, Eleanor, **95**
Roosevelt, Franklin Delano, 68
Rose and Gilbert Tilles Center for the Performing Arts, **13**, 79, **85**, **86**, 106

R *(continued)*
Rosenblatt, Roger, **27**, **34**, **89**, 90
Roy, Robert H., 54
Rubin, Roy, **116**
Ruhmer, Otto, 114

S
Savilon, Marilyn, 75. *See also* LIU, student disability movement
School of Education (Brooklyn), 14
School of Education (C.W. Post), **52**
School of Professional Accountancy, **17**, 79
Schutzer, Paul B'52, **109**
Schwartz, Arnold, 78
Schwartz, Marie, 78
SEAmester, 79, **83**
Seawanaka, 47, 61, **133**
Semel, Terry, 102
Serkin, Peter, 37
Shannon, Raymond, 70
Shenker, Joseph, 90
Sillerman, Laura Baudo, 87, 90, **103**
Sillerman, Robert F.X., 87, 90, **103**
Simon, Paul, 122
Society of Friends (Quakers), 88
Southampton Fire Brigade, **119**
Southampton Hall, **17**
Spector, Robert, 26, **35**, 64, 73
Speech Therapy, **53**
sports. *See* Long Island University sports
Squibb, Edward Robinson, 66
Sroka, Elliot, **97**
Stein, Andrew, 72
Steinberg, David J., **1**, **55**, **83**, **84**, 85-89
Steinberg, Milton, 85
Sternheim, Howard B'54, 66
Stucke, Harry, 73, 74
SUNY Purchase. *See* Westchester Graduate Campus.
Sutton, George, 76
"Swing for Kids," 97
Symbol Technology, 91

T
Taylor, Billy, **27**, **30**, 90
Taylor, James, 122
Tharp, Twyla, 78
Thiele, Fred W., Jr., **108**
Tomorrow Foundation, 87, 103
Tilles, Gilbert, 79, 86
Tilles, Peter, **97**
Tilles, Roger, **97**, 102
Tilles, Rose, **30**, 79, 86
Tucker, Martin, 69, 73
Turner, John, 83
Turner, Tina, 122

INDEX

U
University Hall (Pearl Street, Brooklyn), 60, **61**, 65
University Plaza, 79

V
Van Loen, Alfred, **42**
Verizon, 91

W
Walcott, Gregory D., **51**, 65
Walters, Barbara, 91
Weisel, Elie, **33**
Westchester Graduate Campus at SUNY
  Purchase, **5**, **22**, 57, **82**, 91
White, Sherman, 141
Whitford, Robert C., **47**
Windmill, The, 75, **133**
Winnick Family Foundation, 103
Winnick, Gary P'69, 87, 91 **103**
Winnick, Karen, 87, 91, **103**
WPBX-FM, **20**, **31**, 84
Wolpe, Stefan, **37**, 69-70

Y
Yates, Arthur, 131

Z
Zavitsas, Andreas, 81
Zeckendorf, William, 64, **69**, 70, 84, **94**, 99, **105**
Zeckendorf Health Sciences Center, **24**
Zupko, Arthur, **95**
Zwicker, Charles, 36

*Note 1: Page references in bold represent pages
  with photographs.*
*Note 2: University-specific issues are indexed under
  Long Island University.*

KEY TO ABBREVIATIONS

B	Brooklyn	FW	Friends World	Ph	Pharmacy	S	Southampton	UC	University Center
Br	Brentwood	P	C.W. Post	R	Rockland	UA	University Archives	W	Westchester